Pursuing Purpose

Pursuing Purpose

5 Keys to Fulfilling Your God-Given Purpose

KYRA LANAE

GLORIOUS WORKS PUBLISHING
UPPER DARBY, PENNSYLVANIA

Copyright © 2019 by Kyra Lanae

All rights reserved. This book or any portion thereof may not be reproduced or used in any manner whatsoever without the express written permission of the publisher except for the use of brief quotations in a book review or scholarly journal.

First Printing: 2019

Unless otherwise indicated, all Scripture quotations are taken from the Holy Bible, New Living Translation, copyright © 1996, 2004, 2007, 2013, 2015 by Tyndale House Foundation. Used by permission of Tyndale House Publishers, Inc., Carol Stream, Illinois 60188. All rights reserved. Scriptures marked KJV are taken from the King James Version (KJV): King James Version, public domain. Scriptures marked NIV are taken from the New International Version (NIV): Scripture was taken from The Holy Bible, New International Version ®. Copyright© 1973, 1978, 1984, 2011 by Biblical, Inc.™. Used by permission of Zondervan. Scriptures marked ESV are taken from The Holy Bible, English Standard Version® (ESV®) Copyright © 2001 by Crossway, a publishing ministry of Good News Publishers. All rights reserved. ESV Text Edition: 2016. Scripture quotations taken from the Amplified® Bible (AMP), Copyright © 2015 by The Lockman Foundation. Used by permission. www.Lockman.org

Glorious Works Publishing
201 Bywood Ave. #2214
Upper Darby, PA19082
www.gloriousworkspublishing.com

Special discounts are available on bulk purchases or by corporations, associations, educators, and others. For details, contact publisher at
admin@gloriousworkspublishing.com.
Glorious Works Publishing can bring authors to your live events. For more information or to book an event, contact Glorious Works Publishing at
admin@gloriousworkspublishing.com or visit our website at
www.gloriousworkspublishing.com.

Publisher's Cataloging-In-Publication Data
(Prepared by The Donohue Group, Inc.)

Names: Lanae, Kyra, author.
Title: Pursuing purpose : 5 keys to fulfilling your God-given purpose / Kyra Lanae.
Description: Upper Darby, Pennsylvania : Glorious Works Publishing, [2019] | Includes
    bibliographical references.
Identifiers: ISBN 9781733556507 | ISBN 9781733556521 (ebook)
Subjects: LCSH: Christian life. | Women--Religious life. | Self-actualization (Psychology)
    in women--Religious aspects--Christianity. | Goal (Psychology)--Religious aspects--
    Christianity. | Self-help techniques.
Classification: LCC BV4527 .L36 2019 (print) | LCC BV4527 (ebook) | DDC 248.8/43--
    dc23

Library of Congress Control Number: 2019900986

DEDICATION

To every woman who has wondered what, specifically, she was created for;
To every woman who has yearned for more meaning in her life;
To every woman who has wanted to experience true success and fulfillment;
To every woman who is pursuing purpose;
I dedicate this book to you.

ACKNOWLEDGMENTS

Thank You, God, for creating me with purpose and allowing me to identify and pursue it. Thank You for using me to touch the lives of many, some of whom I will never meet, by creating this resource. My prayer is that in everything that I do, that Your Will be done and that You be glorified.

Thank you to my children, Cameron and Sabrina, who challenged me and encouraged me to complete this project. It is an honor to be your mother. My prayer is that my example of pursuing God and pursuing purpose would drive you to seek after God and His unique purpose for your lives.

Thank you to my exclusive book launch team. Thank you for partnering with me and the vision that God gave to me. My prayer is that your participation in promoting this book ignited a stronger desire in you to pursue your purpose in life.

Thank you to Glorious Works Publishing. May this work that God entrusted to me bring glory back to Him. I pray that each work that you publish brings glory to God.

Thank you to everyone who supported me and everyone who will pick this book up with or without the desire and intention to pursue purpose. I pray that these words will reach you where you are and transform your life forever.

TABLE OF CONTENTS

Introduction 11

Key 1:
Discover Purpose in Your Past and Pain 13
Key 1.1 What was my family life like growing up? 15
Key 1.2 What did my relationships with my peers and authority figures look like? 19
Key 1.3 What events in my life are most memorable and why? 23
Key 1.4 Who inspired me or who have I admired and why? 27
Key 1.5 What questions did I have growing up that I never asked or were never answered? 31
Key 1.6 Who do I need to forgive (myself included) or who do I need to ask for forgiveness? 33
Key 1.7 How can I apply what I have learned about my past to positively change my present and future? 37
Key 1.8 What traumatic or painful experiences have I left unresolved and why have I not sought healing or resolution? 39
Key 1.9 What characteristics do I possess that allow me to overcome my traumatic or painful experiences and who can I confide in or reach out to for support in resolving my traumatic or painful experiences? 41
Key 1.10 How can I help prevent others from experiencing similar painful experiences as myself or help those who have already experienced similar painful experiences? 43

Key 2:
Discover Purpose in Your Position and Posture 45
Key 2.1 What are my expectations for the life stage that I am in right now and how does my reality compare with my expectations? 47
Key 2.2 Where did I acquire my expectations for the life stage that I am in right now? 49

Key 2.3 Why am I working at the company that I am currently working at? 53
Key 2.4 Why do I live where I am currently living? 57
Key 2.5 How can I intentionally, positively impact and be impacted by the people who I frequently encounter? 59
Key 2.6 How do I respond to unfulfilled expectations? 63
Key 2.7 What is my approach to dealing with seemingly difficult people or ideas that differ from my own? 67
Key 2.8 How would those closest to me describe my general outlook on life? 69
Key 2.9 How can I allow my attitude, decisions, and reactions to better reflect the impression that I would like to leave with others? 71

Key 3:
Discover Purpose in Your Personality and Passion 73
Key 3.1 What have I discovered about myself that may come as a surprise to some (including myself)? 75
Key 3.2 What areas of my personality would I change, if I could? 77
Key 3.3 How can I intentionally put forth the time and effort to get to know myself? 81
Key 3.4 What do I find myself talking about most often? 83
Key 3.5 What problems or issues deeply upset me? 87
Key 3.6 What would I spend the majority of my time doing, if money was not an option? 91
Key 3.7 What areas of helping others bring me the most joy? 93
Key 3.8 How can I become a solution to a problem that I'm passionate about? 95

Key 4:
Discover Purpose in Your Potential and Payment 99
Key 4.1 What comes naturally for me? 101
Key 4.2 What motivates me? 103

Key 4.3 What is the biggest hindrance that can prevent me from reaching my fullest potential? 105

Key 4.4 How can I utilize my natural talents, strengths, and motivators to realize the possibilities in my life? 109

Key 4.5 What specific costs of my time, energy and resources have I paid to achieve my goals and fulfill my purpose in life and how much am I willing to pay? 111

Key 4.6 What am I willing to sacrifice in order to achieve my goals? 115

Key 4.7 What is the timeframe that I expect to see a return on my investments of time, energy and resources for my goals and my purpose in life; and how would I respond if I did not receive a return on my investments of time, energy and resources for my goals and my purpose in life? 117

Key 5:
Pursue Your Purpose 119
Key 5.1 Reflect 121
Key 5.2 List 123
Key 5.3 Share 125
Key 5.4 Do 129
Key 5.5 Check 131
Key 5.6 Repeat 133

INTRODUCTION

Welcome to Pursuing Purpose: 5 Keys to Fulfilling Your God-Given Purpose. Pursuing Purpose is a resource that will propel you into discovering and fulfilling your purpose in every area of your life. It will help you identify the purpose of your past, position, and passion among other key identifiers. You will answer questions such as: How can I apply what I have learned about my past to positively change my future? How does my reality compare with my expectations for the life stage that I am in right now? How can I become a solution to a problem that I'm passionate about? How much am I willing to pay of my time, energy and resources to achieve my goals and fulfill my purpose in life?

Pursuing Purpose will also give you practical next steps to take to assist you in seeing the manifestation of your goals, dreams and purpose. It is thought provoking and action inspiring. Whether you are a college student trying to figure out what your next steps are or you are well established in your life and career, but sense that there is more in life waiting for you, Pursuing Purpose is the bridge to help get you from where you are to where you need to be—living a purposeful life.

As you read this book, take your time to digest, reflect and respond to the questions that are designed to probe your heart and mind. In this book I will share examples of my highs, lows, strengths and weaknesses, reflections and discoveries that projected me into living out my purpose. My experiences and responses are simply a guide for you. Provide, analyze and assess your own responses. The more transparent and authentic that you are with yourself as you work your way through this book, the more beneficial it will be to you. Also, take advantage of the accompanying workbook, Pursuing

Purpose Workbook: 5 Keys to Fulfilling Your God-Given Purpose. The workbook is designed to give you ample space to record and reflect on your responses and reinforce and elaborate on key concepts and ideas through worksheets, visuals, schedules, checklists and other resources.

Often, when we hear the idea of finding purpose in our lives, we think singularly, as if there is only one thing that we can or should do in life. The reality is that our purpose in life is to identify what we were created to do and do it in every area of our lives. This book will not only help you to pursue your purpose, but also uncover the hidden purposes in your life. As long as you are living, continue pursuing purpose.

<3 always,

Your sister in Christ,

Kyra Lanae

KEY 1:

DISCOVER PURPOSE IN YOUR PAST AND PAIN

past | noun
1. the time or a period of time before the moment of speaking or writing

pain | noun
1. physical suffering or discomfort caused by illness or injury or mental suffering or distress

Key 1: Discover Purpose In Your Past And Pain

Key 1.1 What was my family life like growing up?

Did you grow up as an only child or were you in a long line of siblings? Were you raised by your parents, grandparents or maybe foster or adoptive parents? Did you have a close-knit extended family or did you grow up only knowing a few family members? What was the atmosphere like in your home? Was it warm, loving and comforting or was it cold and filled with despair?

As you walk down memory lane, deeply think about the mechanics and nuances of your family life. Discovering your past requires you to recall it and begin to dissect it. Subtle things that we overlooked growing up have significance in our lives. Both the unnoticed and profound details help shape who we are and how we perceive and function in our lives several years later.

For example, one of my mentors' mothers died giving birth to him. As heartbreaking as that sounds, it did not stop there. Once his father remarried, within years, his stepmother died. His father's death followed three short years later. As a teenager, his only close relatives, an aunt and uncle ended their lives by murder and suicide. His uncle murdered his aunt before taking his own life. Being bombarded by death, those events absolutely shaped his life and caused him to seek after purpose at a young age.

I have family and friends who were ostracized while growing up because of the belief system that their families ascribed to. Some family members refused to associate with other family members and even shunned them. Due to the isolation and rejection that they experienced, they had to seek comfort, love, and affection elsewhere. At times it led to their demise, but some ultimately found true love in Christ.

Various aspects of our family life can become roadblocks, bridges or even stepping stones in the terrain of our lives. As an adult, I encountered a woman who was a trust fund baby. Her family life and the choices she made were a reflection of the financial security that she had growing up. She did not have access to her trust fund until a certain age, but the knowledge of its existence and stipulations afforded her the freedom to live a certain way. It allowed her to pursue an education and career path of her choice without the daunting question of whether or not her path would lead to financial security.

Our impressions of our family life influence the choices that we make later in life. I met a woman who grew up raising her siblings, so she had no desire to have children. She had a taste of childrearing at a young age and felt that she was all worn out. At times she felt like she missed out on what a real childhood should have been. She mimicked some of the same feelings of the woman who grew up as a latchkey kid. Much of her time was spent alone, taking care of herself. She grew up to be responsible and independent, but there were parts of her childhood that screamed "*adulthood!*"

I cannot forget the woman whose family grew up in poverty. Once she had a little money to her name, she began to give her children and grandchildren all the material things that she could buy. She lacked and was unable to give some of the affection and support that her children could have benefited from, but as long as she bought them what her parents could not afford when she was growing up, she was content. It reminds me of the people who grew up with alcoholic parents. Some of them avoid alcohol at all costs because they witnessed the effects of its abuse; while others indulge in the same behavior even after witnessing the effects of its abuse.

Key 1: Discover Purpose In Your Past And Pain

Whatever the circumstances we found our family life, whether they were favorable or disheartening, they were significant and affected us into adulthood. Dissecting some of those circumstances can help decode the reasoning behind our choices and behaviors.

Now, you answer: What was my family life like growing up?

Key 1.2 What did my relationships with my peers and authority figures look like?

Think back to your middle and high school years. Think about the awkward stages of puberty, peer pressure and transitioning into adulthood. Those years are critical. Were you the one who was sure of who you were and rose above the pressures of teenage years or were you susceptible to the common challenges of trying to be who your friends wanted you to be? Were you bullied or were you a bully or were you neither?

I remember moments of feeling helpless. I remember the drama during those years. There were moments when I wanted someone to save me from it all. Navigating a time when my body, mind, and emotions were rapidly changing was exhausting. It was a time when I felt out of place but so desperately wanted to belong. I had a small core group of friends or rather associates. My mom used to remind me that everyone that smiled in my face was not my friend, not even every one that hung out with me was. I should have clearly seen that and should have known it to be true when something that one person said would turn the whole group against me. It was not only me. We all had our turns of being ostracized. At times it was one of us against the world and other times it was this group against that group.

For whatever reason, one particular summer, the majority of my peers were against a close friend and I. I cannot remember why but I am sure that it was something trivial. There were days when groups of them would follow me home talking, laughing and even throwing things in my direction. I had it all mapped out in my head what exactly I would do if one of them hit me, but the situation never escalated to that point. It not only happened as I walked through my neighborhood. But the taunting continued on the way to school as well. I never shared what was going on with my family or any authority figures. It was just a weird time when I was too old to "run home and tell Mommy" but inside I wanted someone to intervene. During that time, I did not have many authority figures that I could confide in. I was well mannered, so I had seemingly healthy relationships with those in authority but not really the kind that allowed me to open up and trust them enough to invite them into my world.

As an adult, I had the opportunity to be on the other side. I looked at it as coming to the rescue of all the girls involved. While reading at the library, I was surrounded by a group of middle-school-aged girls. One, in particular, was the ringleader. Every chance she had, she spat off something profane or disrespectful. She harassed any peer that was within reach. Several times I asked if she could choose different words to express herself as she colored almost every sentence with profanity. As time went on, it seemed she was no longer getting her fix from insulting those within reach. She proceeded to walk the library, stopping innocent children to berate them. At that point, I had had enough.

I approached the young lady and inquired if I could speak with her. I guess the phrase "do you mind?" still confuses people because she told me that she *did* mind if I spoke with her, so I calmly walked away. Then she followed me and explained that she, in fact, wanted to talk to me and that was why she said yes when I asked if she minded. I followed up with asking her a few questions about herself and what she wants in life. At first, she did not even look at my face. I could tell that the interactions that we were having were not the type that she was accustomed to. The discussion was obviously making her uncomfortable. I began to speak life into her, encourage her and share with her that she did not have to be what she saw around her especially if the majority of what she saw was destructive attitudes and behaviors. Her face lit up, and she even looked in my eyes when we

Key 1: Discover Purpose In Your Past And Pain

began to talk about the joy that life can bring and how her future can be brighter than what she saw at the time. She left our conversation as a different young lady. She was grateful for it, and I am sure that the other young ladies were grateful that someone was attentive and cared enough to come to their rescue.

Often, how we react and interact with others is indicative of how we have acted in the past or how we would have preferred to behave in the past. If you had healthy relationships, it is easier for you to replicate those types of relationships. Conversely, if you did not have healthy relationships, your desire to give what you lacked could override your experiences.

Now, you answer: What did my relationships with my peers and authority figures look like?

Key 1.3 What events in my life are most memorable and why?

Reviewing the chapters in the stories of our lives, some stick out more prominently than others. There are memories that seem to be etched in our hearts forever while others fade away. The ups and downs of life cause some of them to bring back fond memories while others are recollections of unspeakable horror.

One of the joyous memories that I vividly remember was my surprise fifth birthday party. I was wearing my vivid pink, purple and blue striped jacket as I walked into the house filled with food, family, friends, and festivities. That year my family made me a piñata. My mom orchestrated fun and games, and everyone was eagerly engaged. I could not tell you a single gift that I received that day because it was overshadowed by the excitement and appreciation of having a ball with my special guests. It was memorable because that was the only birthday party I remembered having as a child. I felt special and celebrated being surrounded by those who loved me.

I also remember the moment when I thought my heart would explode with pure love and joy. It was the day that my first-born son entered the world. I stood in awe of the wonder of what God created. I never knew that I could love someone as much as I did when I held him in my arms. He was truly a good and perfect gift from God. His sweet face captured my undivided attention and his easy temperament encouraged me to simply sit and watch him be. For extended moments at a time, I simply gazed upon him as he slept.

Up until that point, I spent so much time and energy attempting to receive love from others. In a moment, I shifted my focus from being the recipient to an overabundant giver. My son did not have to do anything to demand my love. It was genuine, free and unconditional. I remember that moment because I got a glimpse of the passion with which God loves his children.

Another memorable moment was not nearly as pleasurable. It was during my teenage years and involved one of my first *real relationships*. Without notice, the guy that I was dating for over a year vanished. He did not vanish off the face of the earth, just out of my world. I was confused, distressed and heartbroken. For months, I tried to get in contact with him and even reached out to his friends hoping to discover something that would make everything make sense. Finally, one day I was standing outside of his friend's house inquiring about him, and he waltzed outside. I thought I would finally receive a reprieve, but I was only met by more distress and rejection.

As he stood before me, he reiterated with his mouth what his behavior screamed. He wanted me to leave him alone. His communication was brief before he returned into the house unbothered. My confusion and pain intensified. Of all the possible tragic scenarios that I had played out in my mind while searching for him, praying to discover a hilarious misunderstanding, this was the most unexpected. I was in shock. I could not, for the life of me, understand why he chose that method of breaking up with me.

I will never forget that memory because of the intense rush of a plethora of negative emotions that I experienced. The grief, frustration, confusion, rejection, anger, and shame erupted from me. I continued to search my mind to determine what I did to deserve such treatment.

Whether wonderful or miserable, we hold on to the memories that we hold on to for a reason. Whether we are conscious of it or subconsciously, those memories affect our worlds. The choices we make, the way that we respond and even some of the beliefs that we hold on to so tightly are tied to our memories.

Now, you answer: What events in my life are most memorable and why?

Key 1: Discover Purpose In Your Past And Pain

Key 1.4 Who inspired me or who have I admired and why?

Who we admire reveals plenty about how we perceive ourselves. Usually, we feel both a level of connection and dissociation with the people we admire. We see a commonality that links us to the person, but at the same time, we see something in them that shows that they have something or are doing something that we are not, or, in some cases, cannot have or do. Being inspired by someone or admiring someone is a balancing act. The key is to acknowledge, commend and draw from their strengths without becoming obsessive or envious.

As a little girl, there were a couple of older girls in my neighborhood and church that I admired. A common theme that I later recognized with them was their inner and outer beauty and other people's positive response to them. Both young ladies were attractive with pretty smiles. Although I did not go to school with them, I just knew that they were the popular girls in their schools. I could tell by the way that I saw people interact with them.

One girl lived in my neighborhood. I watched and admired how the young girls looked up to her, the older girls wanted to be with her, and the older guys wanted to date her. I had the privilege of being around her enough to see how wise she was and enjoy her sense of humor. I wanted to look and feel as poised as she did. I wanted people to flock to me the same way that they did to her.

Another young lady that I admired as a child attended my church. She beamed with inner and outer beauty. She wore confidence on her face. As I watched her involvement in ministry, I witnessed that she was gifted with excelling in administration and was very responsible for her age. She was pleasant, loving and fun to be around. I marveled at the impact that she had on others and the vitality that she brought as she served in ministry. I wanted to be just as important and valued as she appeared to be.

As an adult, I reconnected with both young ladies, and to my surprise, they both shared the impact that I had on them. One came to me for counseling, and the other confided in me after sharing that I was an inspiration to her. I was elated to encourage her by sharing with her that for many years she inspired me and; in fact, I admired her.

With time, the qualities that I admired in people expanded. I later began to admire women that I saw living a life pleasing to God and walking in obedience to His call for them. The details of what they were doing in life did not matter as much as the reason why they were doing it. When I began to see women living out passionate visions that God placed in their hearts, I knew that that was what I wanted for myself. I wanted to be used by God in the unique way that He created especially for me.

One of the women who set a bold example for me started as a mentor and became a friend. As our relationship developed, it became hard to define and compartmentalize our roles in each other's lives, but we were sure that God made our paths cross for a reason. One of the major differences in the woman that I admired as I grew older and the ones that I admired as a little girl was the formation of a relationship. As a little girl, I looked on from afar at the people who inspired me. I did not really know them in depth, rather only by what I could see in passing. By developing a relationship with the woman that inspired me, I was able to see, up close and personal, her strengths as well as her human frailty. It further inspired me because I could identify with her weaknesses and still witness the powerful way that God used her in spite of her human flaws.

Key 1: Discover Purpose In Your Past And Pain

The things we admire in others are the very things that we desire to be pulled out of us or highlighted in us. A part of us knows, deep down within, that it is possible. Witnessing it in others inspires us to discover it in our own lives.

Now, you answer: Who inspired me or who have I admired and why?

Key 1.5 What questions did I have growing up that I never asked or were never answered?

My mom grew up instilled with the notion that "children should be seen and not heard." The idea was that children did not have a voice. They were expected to be respectful, obedient and stay in a child's place. While I agree that children should be respectful, obedient and understand their position as a child, I also believe that children should be recognized as people. People, not only adults, have a desire to be seen, heard, acknowledged and valued. While children may not have the authority to act on every opinion that they have, it should be recognized that they do have an opinion. Even more so, they have questions. There are times when children can be erroneously viewed as disrespectful simply for desiring to gain a better understanding.

Growing up, my family had family meetings. I loved them. My siblings hated them. I thoroughly enjoyed sitting around learning what was going on in our household and what our next steps would be. Each meeting concluded with us asking any questions that we had about the meeting. My siblings rarely spoke up, and I eagerly anticipated asking every single question that I could possibly imagine. I was the youngest, so my siblings were probably annoyed because they already knew the answers. Maybe it bothered them because my extension of the meeting prolonged our dismissal and infringed on their free time.

With each generation, the idea of children speaking, and particularly asking questions has become more acceptable. Now as a parent, I encourage my children to ask questions. It is important for them to understand what is going on and more importantly why something is going on. Any parent of a toddler or even a person who knows a toddler can attest to the barrage of questions that spew out of their mouths. It is not that they are defiant future lawyers. They are merely gaining an understanding of the world around them.

As a parent who has inquisitive children, I still welcome and encourage their questions even after the toddler phase. Along with an openness to ask questions, our family established some rules to balance gaining an understanding and obedience and respect. As a rule, my children are welcome to ask the question *why* but they have to find an appropriate time to ask. When I am giving out an instruction is *not* the appropriate time. We discussed that when they ask at that point, it is because they are gauging whether or not they want to follow the instruction or not and that conflicts with obedience and respect.

Similarly, when my children attended traditional school, I encouraged them to obey those who were in authority—unless they were instructing them to do something wrong—and to wait for an appropriate time to ask any questions about the situation. Situations can quickly escalate when children attempt to give clarification, correct a mistaken adult or even ask a question for understanding after an adult gives an instruction. In an effort to reduce misunderstandings, wisdom is required.

If there were ever any questions that you could not ask growing, think about them and ask now. Ask and find an answer if possible. If there are not any particular questions that you remember having that went unanswered, reflect on whether or not your voice was heard growing up. Were you free to gain an understanding of the world around you?

Now, you answer: What questions did I have growing up that I never asked or were never answered?

Key 1.6 Who do I need to forgive (myself included) or who do I need to ask for forgiveness?

Forgiveness can be a scary thing. The scary thing about forgiveness is that in order to forgive we have to acknowledge unfavorable experiences and mistakes that we might otherwise want buried and expunged from our memories. Forgiveness is humbling, powerful and freeing whether you are in the position to forgive or the position of asking for forgiveness.

One autumn evening, I attended a women's conference, and the speaker mentioned that one important step that some of us needed to take was to give or receive forgiveness. I remembered thinking that I did not have any known areas of unforgiveness in my heart. As much as I could remember, I had forgiven all the people who came to my mind as having previously wronged me. I went through the file cabinet of my heart to see if there was anyone that I needed to forgive. I stood there and invited the Holy Spirit to uncover any unforgiveness in my heart. A rush of emotions overtook me as God brought back to my remembrance a sin that I committed against someone almost twenty years prior. I never asked them for forgiveness, *and* I never forgave myself for it either.

Once the situation was fresh in my mind, I could not simply go on living my life as usual without addressing it. First, I started with forgiving myself. I had to acknowledge what I did was wrong and release myself from the shame and guilt that was attached to my past decisions. I had to admit that I had only made a single mistake and that did not define me as a person or determine the totality of my lifestyle. It was a momentary lapse in reasoning, not a continuation of consecutive bad decisions. After I solidified forgiving myself, it was time to request forgiveness from the other person involved.

Reaching out to ask for forgiveness was a process. It was a sensitive matter, so I wanted to make sure I approached it with care. For weeks I went over how I would approach the person and the situation. I was nervous beyond measure. It was one thing to recount the memory to myself, but speaking it aloud to the other person involved was a different story. When I eventually reached out despite the nerves, I was met by the person's voicemail. We played phone tag for a while, but I did not mind because it bought me a bit more time. It was a catch twenty-two because as much as I wanted to postpone the confrontation, I equally wanted the situation to be over.

When we finally connected on the phone, I began with my apology. As I began to explain what I was apologizing for, the other person probably knew where the conversation was going. It most likely was not an experience that they wanted to relive. Before I could get my complete thought out, the phone disconnected. I did not want to assume the worst, but I could understand why they might have intentionally ended the call. I called back just to be sure. One of the worst things you can do in life is to assume. Was it possible that they did not want to continue the conversation? Yes. And it was just as possible that one of us lost a signal. Once I did not get through a second time, I released myself from the situation knowing that I had done my part in asking for forgiveness. I immediately felt another weight lifted off of me, a weight that I did not even recognize just a few months prior, a weight that I carried for almost twenty years.

When you forgive, you release whoever you are forgiving and that even includes yourself. Humility is required when you extend forgiveness because you admit that you were hurt by a person's actions. When you ask for forgiveness, you humble yourself and admit a fault. Whether or not the other person accepts your apology

Key 1: Discover Purpose In Your Past And Pain

is between them and God. Your freedom comes in knowing that you acknowledged your mistake and attempted to correct it.

Now, you answer: Who do I need to forgive (myself included) or who do I need to ask for forgiveness?

Key 1: Discover Purpose In Your Past And Pain

Key 1.7 How can I apply what I have learned about my past to positively change my present and future?

Our pasts have purpose, and our pasts affect our presents and futures whether we like it or not. Our pasts help shape who we are today and who we aspire to be tomorrow. Our pasts are something that we cannot ignore but rather acknowledge, accept and learn from. If we do not take the necessary steps in properly dealing with our pasts, then we are susceptible to holding on to it and even repeating its mistakes and errors in our presents and futures.

When I reflect on my family life growing up, I can appreciate and replicate the qualities that I believe were beneficial. I have permission to cancel any cycles that are not conducive to the life that I want to experience going forward. I can acknowledge and accept that conditions that were out of my control and even out of my area of understanding affected me.

Recognizing that there were times in my past that I should have reached out for help but did not, I can now reach out unashamed. Along with reaching out for help, I can also be the help that others need even when they are ashamed, afraid or too embarrassed to reach out. When I see someone going through a difficult situation, I can be their respite.

When I find myself going through challenging situations, I will evaluate whether or not the situation triggers a particular response from me because it evokes a memory from my past. I can learn from my past, but I certainly do not need to relive my past. If there are emotions that I am projecting into my present and future because of similar situations from my past, I have to take responsibility over my mind and realize that each situation is independent of each other. I will not respond in the present based off of events from my past.

Where I came from is important but where I am going is more important. When I think about what used to inspire me and what I now admire, I am reminded to look with depth. More so than what can be seen are the things that can be experienced. You can gaze at the beauty of a person, but you can experience the kindness in their hearts. My goal is to admire and attain the tangible characteristics that even a blind person could see.

No matter what the package looks like, I will value each person that I encounter. No one is inferior to me because of their age, ability, reputation or status. God uniquely and creatively created each of us and I am honored to have the privilege to engage with His marvelous creation.

Even if there are times—correction when there are times—that I make mistakes, I will be quick to acknowledge and address it. I will give myself the freedom to forgive myself, understanding that I will never reach perfection on this side of heaven. Likewise, no one else will reach perfection here on earth, so I also need to be ready to forgive and ask for forgiveness.

My mistakes were not in vain. They were learning experiences. My past was not in vain, and neither is yours.

Now, you answer: How can I apply what I have learned about my past to positively change my present and future?

Key 1.8 What traumatic or painful experiences have I left unresolved and why have I not sought healing or resolution?

It is sometimes comforting to tuck it away, to lock it in the closet or sweep it under the rug. The only caveat is that the rug begins to bulge. If you decide not to deal with your traumatic or painful experiences, eventually, in one way or another they will deal with you. You may be able to stand in front of the closet door for ten, twenty or thirty or more years but at some point, the hinges will weaken, beginning to creak, and the very things that you tried so desperately to hold back in secrecy will burst out and become exposed. The Bible says, "For all that is secret will eventually be brought into the open, and everything that is concealed will be brought to light and made known to all" (Luke 8:17).

The most common reasons for concealing a traumatic or painful experience are shame, fear, and the torment of reliving the experience. The Word of God and godly counsel guides us in the healing process. Shame thrives in secrecy and fear lives in the unknown. 1 John 4:18 says, "There is no fear in love, but perfect love casts out fear. For fear has to do with punishment, and whoever fears has not been perfected in love." When we confront fear by embracing the love of God and the truth of His Word, we can move past our fears to receive the healing that we need. The beautiful thing about healing from a traumatic or painful experience is that it does not stop with you. Once you receive healing from a particular issue, it frees you up to extend healing to others involved in similar situations. That is what Paul was talking about in 2 Corinthians 1: 3-4 (NIV):

Praise be to the God and Father of our Lord Jesus Christ, the Father of compassion and the God of all comfort, who comforts us in all our troubles, so that we can comfort those in any trouble with the comfort we ourselves receive from God.

For me, the traumatic situation that I thought would accompany me to my grave was the rape that I experienced. After it happened, I thought I could sweep it under the rug and pretend that it never happened. I did not make it through an entire year before I was faced with the reality that covering up what happened to me would not negate the fact that it happened. My main reason for choosing not to initially deal with the situation was the immense amount of shame that I felt. I was in disbelief that it happened to me and I was even more shameful because I felt that it was my fault. Side note—if you ever experience rape, it is not your fault.

When I finally got to the place where I could not withhold my secret any longer, I confided in a trusted party who was able to give me godly wisdom and an empathetic heart because they had similar experiences. When I spoke it aloud and was met with love, understanding, empathy, and comfort, it dispelled the lies and fear that the enemy whispered into my mind about exposing my experience. I found freedom!

As long as our trauma and pain are buried inside of us, it has the power to torment us on demand. When we expose the trauma and pain, we give ourselves the opportunity to heal. It is similar to a bandaged wound that is never permitted to breathe. There is comfort in covering up the wound, but it will never heal properly under those conditions.

Now, you answer: What traumatic or painful experiences have I left unresolved?

Key 1: Discover Purpose In Your Past And Pain

Key 1.9 What characteristics do I possess that allow me to overcome my traumatic or painful experiences and who can I confide in or reach out to for support in resolving my traumatic or painful experiences?

We were created in the image of God. That means that He has placed the characteristics that He has within us. God has equipped us to withstand the trauma and pain that life can bring by resting in Him and growing in our identity in Him. Because of the sacrifice of Jesus Christ, we have power and authority over the plans of the enemy and the traumatic and painful things that he brings into our lives to destruct us.

The most powerful weapon that we have against evil is love, God's love. When I looked at experiencing rape, my natural response was not love. As I began to submerge myself in the love that God had for me and inquire of how God wanted me to resolve the situation, I was able to address it with love. Love helped heal my wounds as well as the wounds of the young man involved.

The picture of love that I was able to extend was the same love that I received from God. When I was stuck in my sin and an enemy of God, he sent his Son, Jesus Christ to die for me. It was not fair, but He did it anyway. He did it because of love. He did not do it because I deserved it but purely because of love. So, when I evaluated the situation, I realized that society would say I should rightly prosecute and seek justice, but I viewed it through the lens of love. When I extended love and confronted the young man with a trusted third party and forgave him, I was able to extend mercy. Mercy is what God showed all of us when we justly should have been punished.

Another characteristic that motivated and assisted me in seeking resolution was my desire to help people. When I realized that my healing in that area would allow me to help others going through similar situations, I knew that I could not continue to stuff it under the rug.

Along with confronting the person who participated in my traumatic situation, I sought godly counsel from my pastors. I was not opposed to therapists or psychologists, but that was not the path of resources that God led me to. I am a firm believer that God can and does bring about healing through the use of medical professionals; however, He is not limited to them. The best course of action is to prayerfully seek His Will regarding your situation. The key is to reach out to someone. Do not keep the trauma and pain bottled up. There is no healing in hiding; only torment, fear and shame exist there.

Now, you answer: What characteristics do I possess that allow me to overcome my traumatic or painful experiences and who can I confide in or reach out to for support in resolving my traumatic or painful experiences?

Key 1.10 How can I help prevent others from experiencing similar painful experiences as myself or help those who have already experienced similar painful experiences?

We are not God, and we do not hold every situation in our hands, but we do have the ability to help prevent others from experiencing similar painful experiences that we have encountered. Even if we are not able to help prevent a situation, we can be available to help in the event that a situation does arise.

A few ways that I can help prevent others from experiencing traumatic situations are to be open, honest, attentive and available. Revelation 12:11 says that we overcome by our testimony. Being open and honest about what I have experienced and what God has done in my life can serve as a loving warning or deterrent for others to avoid some of the situations that I found myself in. It also serves others who have unfortunately already experienced a traumatic situation. It gives hope and can point them in the direction of healing. Knowing that someone else went through what they went through and are still standing can encourage them to seek love and healing, with the confidence that it is available for them.

When I first confided in someone about the rape that I experienced, one of the first things they did was open up and honestly share with me their similar experience. I saw where they currently were in their life, and it gave me hope knowing that I could get past what I had experienced. It showed me that God could still use me; in fact, He would use that very situation to bring glory to Himself and to help me and help others.

Along with being open and honest, I can devote my time and attention to others to help prevent them from experiencing similar painful experiences like I did or help those who have already gone through similar painful experiences to recover and heal. When I experience something, it gives me insight on that particular situation. When I see others who showed signs of distress or signs that they are heading in the same direction, I can lovingly be open, honest and available to them. It would require me to be attentive to them. At times, we can get so caught up in our own worlds that we lack sensitivity and attentiveness to those around us. When this happens, we become deaf to their silent cries for help, and we miss an opportunity to reach out and soothe their pain. In extreme cases, we might even miss an opportunity to save their lives.

Being available is crucial. The enemy loves isolation. One of the ways that he precipitates torment in people's lives is through isolation. That is why it is vital to reach out when you need help. When people take steps to reach out, it is imperative that there is someone available for them to reach out to. I can now be that person who is available. I may not have all of the answers or resources, but I can be available to give them what I can and point them in the direction of receiving more.

It is not our job to save people. Only Jesus can do that. However, we do have the ability to help prevent traumatic situations and support others after the fact.

Now, you answer: How can I help prevent others from experiencing similar painful experiences as myself or help those who have already experienced similar painful experiences?

KEY 2:

DISCOVER PURPOSE IN YOUR POSITION AND POSTURE

po•si•tion | noun

1. a place where someone or something is located or has been put

pos•ture | noun

1. a particular way of dealing with or considering something; an approach or attitude

Key 2: Discover Purpose In Your Position And Posture

Key 2.1 What are my expectations for the life stage that I am in right now and how does my reality compare with my expectations?

As we go through life, we have expectations of what our lives should look like at various stages. While it is wise to have a plan and a sense of direction, we have to remember that we do not hold the master blueprint to our lives. Everything will not always pan out the way that we expect them to.

I remember when I was a teenager, my plans in life were to become an obstetrician, get married at eighteen years old, and have three children by the age of twenty-five. I had it all mapped out. When I realized that I did not have the desire to attend college and medical school for several years after high school, I tossed that profession out the window. I held on to the expectation that I would marry young and start a family shortly after.

I got married and started a family at nineteen years old, and by then I decided to become a labor and delivery nurse. I always loved pregnancy, labor, delivery, and babies. I figured that the schooling would not be as long and I would still get the opportunity to play an intricate role in taking care of women and their babies. Once I realized that I would have to actually go through nursing school and possibly see crazy emergency room horror stories, I tossed that profession out of the window as well.

In my early twenties, I got divorced and settled into the career path of childcare administration. At one point, I believed that I would eventually own and operate my own childcare center. That desire to help women and their babies was still there, but I fell in love with the administrative side of my job. In my early twenties, I thought that I was finally on track to starting a career and not simply working a job. Shortly after, I knew that God placed entrepreneurship inside of me and for years I tried starting this business and that business. At one point I had about six different business cards. Nothing took off quite as I expected it to. Each season that I approached came with different expectations.

My current expectation is being in the Will of God, being obedient to Him, no matter what that looks like. It does not come easy, and I will not even pretend that it does not come with unique challenges. In my head, if I am not careful, I can easily get sucked into clinging to expectations that come from my selfish desires. It is a natural expectation to expect the business that I own to flourish because of the time, energy and resources that I put into it. It is also a natural expectation to expect that as I approach thirty years old that I would remarry and continue having children because, well, I'm a catch. My life currently does not align with what my natural expectations would be for this stage in my life, but because I choose to place my expectation in Christ, my reality always reflects His perfect expectations for my life.

Proverbs 16:9 reminds us that, "We can make our plans, but the Lord determines our steps." Knowing this truth and holding on to it will help our realities match our expectations.

Now, you answer: What are my expectations for the life stage that I am in right now and how does my reality compare with my expectations?

Key 2: Discover Purpose In Your Position And Posture

Key 2.2 Where did I acquire my expectations for the life stage that I am in right now?

We live in a society that bombards us with messages, ideologies, and expectations that, if we are not careful, we can take on as our own. While our selfish desires can influence our expectations, the things and people around us can play a part in us acquiring expectations for our lives. James 4:1-3 speaks to both the desires in us and the focus that we place on what we see around us, in others.

What is causing the quarrels and fights among you? Don't they come from the evil desires at war within you? You want what you don't have, so you scheme and kill to get it. You are jealous of what others have, but you can't get it, so you fight and wage war to take it away from them. Yet you don't have what you want because you don't ask God for it. And even when you ask, you don't get it because your motives are all wrong—you want only what will give you pleasure. (James 4:1-3)

One of the things that I am grateful for is that I did not grow up in the age of the social media craze. Social media was just beginning to take off when I was in high school, but it was not nearly what it is today. To this day, it is still an area in which I have to guard my heart. It is too easy to get swept away in social media land, comparing my life to thousands of people, some who I do not even know. If I am not careful, my expectations can become manipulated by the filtered highlight reel of a stranger's life. I take advantage of the benefits of social media in regards to having a social media presence while running my business, but even with that I still take breaks from time to time. It helps me to combat the temptation of developing anxiety and having unrealistic expectations based on the constant barrage of displays from other people's lives.

Having people's lives and our every desire just a click away can tempt us to create expectations for our own lives from what we see around us, but it is not the only way. Some can attest to their expectations being modeled after the expectations of the people closest to them. At times it can present itself as a family member or significant other. Maybe it looks like the artiste who came from a line of corporate business leaders or the homemaker who is being encouraged to chase a career in a time when many people are screaming blind support for the feminist movement.

Once upon a time, I never imagined being a stay-at-home mom. I actually dreaded the idea. At one point, I had an opportunity to stay home, and I volunteered for six to eight hours a day. It was not until I began to shift my expectations to God's expectations for my life that I began to embrace the idea of being home with my children. At that time, my children were not yet school-age, and it was a momentary experience. Little did I know, it was simply a trial run for what was to come. Years later, a close friend of mine mentioned that she could see me traveling the world preaching the gospel and *homeschooling* my children.

I banned her from even speaking that out of her mouth. I did not want her giving God any ideas. I did not have a single ounce of desire to homeschool my children. One of my favorite verses in the Bible is Psalms 37:4, which states, "Delight yourself in the Lord, and he will give you the desires of your heart" (ESV). I always thought that scripture meant that if I delight in the Lord, then He would give me whatever I wanted. To an extent, God does give us the things that we desire, but there is another side to that verse. The more that we delight in God, the more our desires began to reflect His desires. It is like He comes in and replaces our selfish desires with His desires for our lives. Within three to four months, I was praying for God to make a way for me to be able to one day homeschool my children. Almost a year after I prayed that prayer, I began homeschooling.

As I submit my will to God's will, my reality mirrors my life's expectations more closely because the source that I gain my expectations from is the source and orchestrator of the universe and everything in it. We have to be aware of where we acquire our expectations for our lives. Go to the creator of life Himself.

Now, you answer: Where did I acquire my expectations for the life stage that I am in right now?

Key 2: Discover Purpose In Your Position And Posture

Key 2.3 Why am I working at the company that I am currently working at?

The most obvious response to why we work where we do could be that we needed a job, and the company needed an employee and so the two came together and "Voilà!" However, the truth, although not so popular, is that you are working where you are because there's a specific reason why you should be there. In fact, the exact position you presently occupy was given to you for a purpose. God does not do anything by chance or mistake. He is purposeful in all that He does. That includes sending you to the company that you currently work for.

In the past, I knew that God placed me at my places of employment for a reason. One particular time, God gave me an in-depth assignment before I even started in my position. When I went for the interview, I assumed that it would be business as usual. They asked me questions; I answered; I asked them questions, and they answered in turn. After I was offered the position, I requested a meeting to pick up any personnel materials that I would need so that I could get acclimatized to the company as I awaited my start date. To my surprise, at the meeting that I requested, my soon-to-be boss asked if I minded accepting a management position instead of the assistant position for which I applied, was interviewed and got hired. She mentioned that she wanted to give me a voice on the management team. She also asked if I minded her bumping up my salary and adding a few more hours a week so that I would qualify for all of the company benefits. I conceded.

After reveling in the obvious favor that I was shown, I toured the company. While on tour, God began to *assign* people to me. Before my first day, I clearly knew the specific purpose and people that God sent me to that company for. I was sent to be a light in a dark place.

John 1:5 says, "The light shines in the darkness, and the darkness can never extinguish it." My boss must have read Matthew 5:14-16 because my office was positioned where almost every person in the company encountered me on a daily basis.

You are the light of the world—like a city on a hilltop that cannot be hidden. No one lights a lamp and then puts it under a basket. Instead, a lamp is placed on a stand, where it gives light to everyone in the house. In the same way, let your good deeds shine out for all to see, so that everyone will praise your heavenly Father. (Matthew 5:14-16)

I greeted and engaged everyone with love and joy. It simply burst from me. It did not matter who they were or how they were. I knew in advance that God placed me there to fill that place with His radiance. I extended love to those who approached my office including a colleague who openly adorned their belongings with 666 and wore human teeth as jewelry. And that was not even the person who was coined as the most irreligious person in the place. Ironically, the allegedly most secular person that I encountered would often stop in my office just to appreciate me for being a burst of sunshine when they came to work. That same individual witnessed a situation where I was not treated justly and was blown away, saying, "They treat you like [crap] and you still only have positive things to say about them and the situation."

When she finally inquired about how I did it, I was able to share Christ with her. She was apprehensive. I vividly remember her response. She said, "I don't know about all that Jesus stuff but..." I reminded her that for the length of time that she knew me, I was never forceful with my faith, but if she wanted to know how I lived the way that I did, I had to tell her the truth. It was JESUS, all JESUS!

Key 2: Discover Purpose In Your Position And Posture

I will never forget the day that one of the young ladies that God *assigned* to me poured out her heart to me and confessed that she knew that I was sent to that company for her. I jokingly said, "Yeah, I know." From there, I was able to share with her *how* I knew. It opened up the conversation for us to discuss her salvation.

My paycheck and benefits were just a bonus. Your paycheck and benefits are just a bonus. There is a purpose in the place where you are planted.

Now, you answer: Why am I working at the company that I am currently working at?

Key 2: Discover Purpose In Your Position And Posture

Key 2.4 Why do I live where I am currently living?

Where do you lay your head down at night? It may be in your dream home or maybe your starter home. Maybe the place that you call home is a temporary rental or even just a room in someone else's home. Wherever you currently are, there is a purpose for you being there. You may not even know the magnitude of your presence. The very thing that bothers you about where you are may possibly play an essential role in your purpose for being there.

When I moved into my apartment, one of the first things I discovered was the paper-thin walls. I did not know initially, but it was strangely brought to my attention. I was vocal as I worshipped God through singing at home. Unbeknownst to me, my private time with God was not exactly *private*. One day, a neighbor approached me inquiring if I spoke in tongues. I thought it was a rather odd question, but I replied. My neighbor went on to tell me that they could hear me and began to share their family's religious background and practices with me. As I walked away, so many things flashed through my mind. I tried to recount all of the intimate conversations that were most likely intercepted. I made a mental note to attempt to keep my voice down. My journal became a close friend.

The longer I stayed in my apartment, the more my neighbors approached me. I never received a complaint, only encouragement, and affirmations. Various people began to inquire if I was the one singing all the time. I was guilty. I sang constantly. Neighbors from the farthest parts of the building mentioned that they could hear me from their apartments. I did not understand how that could be, but I realized that my time of worshipping the Lord echoed throughout my building and that was profound.

One of the best encounters that I had was on an ordinary Tuesday morning. I was singing and listening to a spontaneous worship set when I heard something rattle at my apartment door. I typically did not welcome interruptions when I spent time with God, but I was led to go to the door to check it out. I glanced out of my peephole and saw a woman standing at my door with her hand raised. It was difficult to grasp what she was doing so I resumed worshipping and began praying. Again, I was led back to the door. This time I opened it only to discover an empty hallway.

A few moments later, the woman reappeared with tears streaming down her face. She explained that when she came to my door to give me a flyer, she heard the songs through the door. As soon as she heard "The blood of Jesus" she was overwhelmed and began to worship God outside of my door. We continued to talk and minister to one another. We even exchanged contact information. She revealed that she planned on not coming to my building that day but something told her to come and she needed to encounter God at that moment. Within months following our encounter, she went home to be with the Lord.

Those interactions with relative strangers shifted my mindset about my modest apartment with its paper-thin walls. I was grateful for the very thing that was initially a nuisance. What have you overlooked or complained about as it relates to where you live that God sees purpose in? It could be the neighborhood that you are desperately attempting to escape but inevitably find yourself. There are people in that place waiting for you to identify your purpose for being there.

Now, you answer: Why do I live where I am currently living?

Key 2: Discover Purpose In Your Position And Posture

Key 2.5 How can I intentionally, positively impact and be impacted by the people who I frequently encounter?

Can we agree on the fact that God is intentional? Every person that we encounter is there for a reason. Those whom we encounter frequently, whether at work, where we live, at church or even the grocery store are divinely connected to us. You might think that God would not be concerned about something as trivial as orchestrating every encounter that we have with someone, but might I remind you that Matthew 10:30 says that each hair on our heads has a number. Now, that is what I call caring about the tiniest details. So, now that we agree that those people are in our lives for a reason, what can we do about it?

One of the easiest things that I began to do to intentionally impact people was to engage them. Something as simple as saying hello or asking how a person is doing can impact them tremendously. A few times my children asked why I continued to smile and say hello to people even when most people did not respond. I reminded them that a smile or greeting could change someone's life. I know it might sound too easy or insignificant, but the reality is, you never know who was contemplating taking their life but reconsidered it when they were simply acknowledged by you.

I once viewed an interview of a young man who helped save someone's life unintentionally. He befriended a young lady and occasionally listened to her when she had issues going on in her life. One day, he read a poem that he wrote simply for her feedback. After he finished, she shared that she was tempted to commit suicide, but after hearing what he said in his poem, she decided not to. While he did not know what was going on in her mind and heart in those moments, he previously made a decision to value her by simply engaging with her.

As I consciously choose to engage with people, I do not stop with a greeting and a smile. I am known for inviting strangers over to my house. Neighbors, co-workers, visitors from church or even strangers; I do not limit my hospitality to my family and friends. When I open up my home to others, I invite them into my world. It is not a time for me to mask who I am and how I really live. Rather, they have an opportunity to see me live out my *real* life.

At one point, I welcomed a little girl into my home for six months. I was her caretaker in the evenings and overnight. While she was in my home, she became an addition to our family. When my children received a "salary" for their chores, so did she. When I read the bible, prayed with, kissed my children and told them that I loved them before bed, I did the same with her. In the same way that I gave my children individualized attention and had movie nights with just a party of two or took them out individually for a special dinner, I did the same with her. I was honored to have the opportunity to intentionally pour love into her.

Even now, I still open up my home regularly in order to connect with people. Weekly, I invite a young lady over for dinner and games. Our family loves playing games, so chances are if you come over, we will either end up playing a game or attempt to teach or tell you about a game. One of the things that I keep in mind is that God can use something as minute as board games to be a bridge to relationships, help, and healing.

I cannot pretend that the benefits of what I do are not mutual. God is amazing like that! When he connects people, it is for the benefit of both parties involved. While I have the privilege of extending love through hospitality, I also receive encouragement and joy from brightening someone's day. When we encounter people, it

Key 2: Discover Purpose In Your Position And Posture

is for a purpose. They have the opportunity to impact us, and we have the opportunity to impact them.

Now, you answer: How can I intentionally, positively impact and be impacted by the people who I frequently encounter?

Key 2.6 How do I respond to unfulfilled expectations?

If you have lived for any amount of time, you can concur that things do not always go as planned. We learn that truth at a very young age. How we respond to unfulfilled expectations deals greatly with our perspective. If we think about when toddlers have unfulfilled expectations, in many cases, it results in a tantrum. At that age, their perspective is highly self-centered. Unfortunately, toddlers are not the only ones who can fall victim to a self-centered perspective. The truth is that our very nature is self-centeredness. That is why it is vital to renew our minds and take on God's perspective.

Romans 12:2 reminds us, "And do not be conformed to this world [any longer with its superficial values and customs], but be transformed *and* progressively changed [as you mature spiritually] by the renewing of your mind [focusing on godly values and ethical attitudes], so that you may prove [for yourselves] what the will of God is, that which is good and acceptable and perfect [in His plan and purpose for you]" (AMP). It takes time and effort to fill your mind with God's perspective so that when your expectations are unfulfilled, you do not respond with a tantrum.

When we have God's perspective, we can address disappointments with hope and joy. At times it may take some encouragement to remind yourself, but the key is to quickly remember. Remind yourself that God causes all things to work together for the good of those who love Him and are called according to His purpose. That became one of my life verses when I began to take on God's perspective. When my son, who was only eight years old at the time, was suicidal, I reminded him and myself of God's Word. During that time, I began to reflect on the many times that God already turned horrible things around for good in my life. It was from that situation that my first book, *Beauty for Ashes: The Transformation of my Life's Darkest Moments* was born.

Through *Beauty for Ashes*, God allowed me to touch lives all over the world. I never anticipated that I would connect with women in South Africa or hear someone tell me that my book, which highlights God's awesomeness in my life, is the buzz *on another continent*. That was just *part* of what God caused to work together for my good. Shortly after surrendering the situation over to God, my son's life changed drastically. He became happy and healthy in no time. Every clinical issue that was found at the initial evaluation vanished before his extended assessments were even completed.

The irony about unfulfilled expectations is that they open the door for unexpected fulfillment. When God closes a door or allows an unfulfilled expectation in our lives, it is because He has a grander plan that we simply cannot see in that moment. I once heard someone compare our perspective versus God's perspective of our lives to a child sitting and watching her mother stitching a piece of material. From where the little girl was sitting, she could only see the underside of the material. If you are familiar with sewing, embroidery or other forms of needlework, you know that the underside is not nearly as pretty as the front or top portion. So, from the little girl's perspective, it was difficult to see what her mother was making. It was not until her mother invited her up on her lap to see the work of art from her perspective that the little girl was able to understand and appreciate its beauty.

God is working out all of our unfulfilled expectations into a masterpiece, but we will never understand it or appreciate it if we continue to view it from our perspective. Prior to my son's situation, I certainly did not expect to leave a job that I loved as soon as I did. Had I not left my job, I would not have started my journey as an

Key 2: Discover Purpose In Your Position And Posture

author, publisher and I most definitely would not be a homeschooling mom. Both ministries of being an author, and publisher and a homeschool supervisor were aspects of God's purpose for my life that I could have never predicted. And I love them both. Isaiah 55:8-9 reminds us that God's ways and thoughts are higher than our own. Do not become so fixated on your expectations that you miss out on what God is doing in your life.

Now, you answer: How do I respond to unfulfilled expectations?

Key 2.7 What is my approach to dealing with seemingly difficult people or ideas that differ from my own?

In order to approach this question, think of the sandpaper people and ideas in your life. If you are wondering what sandpaper people or ideas are, they are the people or ideas that rub you the wrong way. How do you feel when you encounter them? Do you get frustrated or stressed out? Do you take it as an opportunity to evaluate your posture? Posture is a particular way of dealing with or considering something; it is an approach or attitude.

So now, shift your focus back to you. Did you know that seemingly difficult people or ideas that differ from your own are blessings in disguise? Of course, the sandpaper feels rough and uncomfortable but think about the purpose of sandpaper. Sandpaper is paper with an abrasive (usually sand) stuck to it, used for smoothing or polishing woodwork or other surfaces. The purpose of using something coarse is to buff out the imperfections. If you tried to sand a piece of wood with a smooth piece of paper, nothing would happen. The same is true with us. We need "coarse" people and ideas to challenge us and perfect us.

Dealing with seemingly difficult people can benefit us in more than one way if we posture ourselves correctly. Instead of harboring frustration when dealing with a seemingly difficult person, focus on what areas you can grow in because of your interactions with them. Maybe you need to grow in patience. James 1:2-4 reminds us, "Dear brothers and sisters, when troubles of any kind come your way, consider it an opportunity for great joy. For you know that when your faith is tested, your endurance has a chance to grow. So, let it grow, for when your endurance is fully developed, you will be perfect and complete, needing nothing."

Maybe you have impeccable patience and kindness, but you need to grow in boldness. Seemingly difficult people or ideas that differ from your own can challenge you in that regard as well. At one point, I worked with someone who was a bit intimidating and dealing with them stirred up boldness in me. I did not become overly confrontational, but I became more and more comfortable standing up for myself and those who I represented. It challenged me to walk boldly into the leadership position that I was called to occupy. If every colleague that I encountered was sweet as pie or we never had a conflict, I would not have been able to exercise the muscle that I needed to, in order to be an effective leader.

Another area in which ideas that differ from your own can assist is helping you to better understand and support your own ideas. Opposing ideas have the benefit of challenging you to evaluate why you support the things that you support. I have a friend who always tries to look at any situation from the opposing position. It does not necessarily have to be the way that she feels about a situation, but she looks at it from various angles. She is naturally gifted at doing that. For those of us who are not naturally gifted to view ideas in that regard, when people present us with another way of thinking about a situation, we can benefit from it.

There is purpose in opposition. Seemingly difficult people can cause us to grow. Differing ideas are a necessary challenge. It does not feel good in that moment, but in the end, you become better. It is all about how you approach them.

Now, you answer: What is my approach to dealing with seemingly difficult people or ideas that differ from my own?

Key 2.8 How would those closest to me describe my general outlook on life?

One of the benefits of having a community is that you have people around you that you can experience life with. Hopefully, there are a few people who are close enough to see the real you—not the social media, filters, perfect lighting, best angles, fake smiles, "I love life, and my life is great *all the time*"—you! So, if those closest to you were asked about you, what would they say? No one is perfect, and we all have areas to grow in, but would those closest to you describe your general outlook on life as positive or negative?

There always seems to be a debate on what constitutes a positive disposition or outlook on life versus being fake and unrealistic. I believe the line can be drawn by evaluating what is done behind closed doors. That is why those closest to you, who actually see you up close and personal would be better candidates to describe your general outlook on life, as opposed to the thousands of people that follow you on social media.

A positive outlook on life looks for the best, believes for the best and hopes for the best. It does not mean that you ignore reality or live in La-La Land. It simply means that despite what the reality is, you choose to look at the positives instead of sulking about the negatives. A part of looking at the positives in life is finding solutions to problems when they arise instead of complaining about them. While some people may naturally have a more positive disposition, being positive is a choice.

No matter what I go through in life, I choose the way that I respond to it. It certainly does not mean that I do not have feelings or emotions, but I choose not to let my feelings and emotions control me. The anchor that allows me to continue to choose joy over and over again is the hope that I have in Christ. Proverbs 10:28 says, "The hope of the righteous [those of honorable character and integrity] is joy," (AMP). Romans 15:13 answers the question of how I have the joy that produces a positive outlook on life. "I pray that God, the source of hope, will fill you completely with joy and peace because you trust in him. Then you will overflow with confident hope through the power of the Holy Spirit" (Romans 15:13). The reason is that I trust in God.

God, who is the very author of life, holds everything in the palm of His hands. My posture is that, if God allows something to happen, it is for a purpose that greatly outweighs the damage. I remember back when one of my engagements were broken off, I was heartbroken. It took months for me to get over it, which was a long time for me. I wanted to uproot my entire life and move just to start over. That happened before I found my identity in Christ. It was actually that very situation that caused me to pursue God. I remember a wise woman telling me that my situation did not take God by surprise. Even years later, I remind myself of those words when life takes me on a turn that I do not expect or agree with. The fact is that a broken heart, which was extremely painful, drove me straight into the arms of God. That was just the beginning. Now that I have more experience with God's faithfulness, I cling to Him, trusting that He can turn every negative thing into a positive event.

Personality aside, is your posture positive or negative? You do not have to smile nonstop or become a bubbly ball of cheer to look at life with joy. Joy is also described as great pleasure and enjoyment. Why would you want to turn that down?

Now, you answer: How would those closest to me describe my general outlook on life?

Key 2: Discover Purpose In Your Position And Posture

Key 2.9 How can I allow my attitude, decisions, and reactions to better reflect the impression that I would like to leave with others?

Each day, we make choices. In fact, we make so many choices that we are not even conscious of some of the choices that we make. The key to allowing your attitude, decisions, and reactions to better reflect the impression that you would like to leave others with is to make conscious choices going in that direction. Of course, it is easier said than done, but it starts with a choice.

For several years, I wore my hair in the same two hairstyles almost every single day. I dyed my hair blond, and for years I faithfully wore it in one curly puff on top of my head or all out with a headband. I admired other hairstyles on other people, but I stuck with my good ole faithful hairstyles. I remember I used to compliment other people on their beautiful hairstyles. Despite appreciating a hairstyle, I did not attempt to wear my hair differently. In my eyes, it was not for me. I had a similar experience when it came to clothing. I dressed in one particular style although I found other styles attractive. I used to say that those styles were nice, but again, it was not for me.

One day, I finally realized that I was the only person putting limits on myself. No one told me that I could not change my hairstyle or dress differently. When I received the revelation that I was free to make my own choices in regards to appearance, without unnecessarily restraining myself, I ran with it. I finally chose to do something different and did it. I began switching up my hairstyles as often as I desired to. Now, it is hard for people to pin down my look. I have even had people reintroduce themselves two and three times because they did not recognize me. I began to wear varied styles of clothing depending on my preference for the day. It was not a matter of me trying to be someone that I was not, but rather choosing to embrace the things that I desired but somehow determined that it was not fit for me.

The point of saying all of this is to show you that if you desire to make adjustments to your attitude, decisions, and reactions to better reflect the impression that you would like to leave with others, then determine what you would like to see and make a conscious choice to pursue it. Years ago, when I worked in childcare, I realized that I had more patience with the children that I interacted with in the childcare center than I had with my own children. Once I realized that fault, I knew that it was not something that I wanted to continue to see in my life. I then made a conscious decision to extend even more patience and kindness to my children when I returned home from work. It took practice, but I had to continue to consciously choose the new direction that I wanted to go in every day.

Making changes are typically not the easiest thing to do, but they always start with a choice and are followed up with action. It is not enough to say how you would like to see yourself in life. You have to follow through with the necessary actions to bring about that change.

Now, you answer: How can I allow my attitude, decisions, and reactions to better reflect the impression that I would like to leave with others?

KEY 3:

DISCOVER PURPOSE IN YOUR PERSONALITY AND PASSION

per•son•al•i•ty | noun

1. the combination of characteristics or qualities

pas•sion | noun

1. an intense desire or enthusiasm for something

Key 3: Discover Purpose In Your Personality And Passion

Key 3.1 What have I discovered about myself that may come as a surprise to some (including myself)?

How much time have you taken to get to know yourself? I mean *really* get to know yourself. Sometimes we go through life just going through the motions or following the crowd and not taking the necessary steps to actually get to know who we are or what we like. When you become intentional about discovering various parts of your personality, you will be able to be authentically you.

For a long time, I did not know much about myself. For many years, I jumped from relationship to relationship. As a result, I never took the time to get to know who I was or what I enjoyed apart from the person I was in the relationship with. I was consumed with them and our relationship. If *they* were a sports fan, *we* were sports fans. If *they* enjoyed rap music, *we* enjoyed rap music. Most of my leisure time was spent with my significant other, and I felt that I often needed to compromise who I was for the sake of the relationship. The truth is that for many years I did not even know who I was.

It was not until my mid-twenties when I decided to take a break from pursuing romantic relationships that I took the time to get to know myself. Most of my time initially was spent getting to know who God was and who I was in Him. I began to see myself as a valuable prize. Aside from getting to know how God felt about me, I began to see the little things that brought me joy. I began to read again, a joy that I used to have as a child but somehow faded away. I realized how much I enjoy painting. I discovered my love for jazz.

One of the biggest personality discoveries I had was discovering that I am actually an introvert. For most of my life, I had considered myself an extrovert, then I moved to an ambivert and eventually realized that I am an introvert. I believe I was born with a gift of gab.

I would talk to anyone. When I started, I did not stop. As a child, my mom used to tell me that just because there was silence, it did not mean that I had to fill it with talking. Because I enjoyed engaging with people, I never once thought that I could possibly be an introvert.

What I learned was that introverts are not necessarily off, hiding under a rock somewhere. There are actually different types of introverts. I happened to be a social introvert, one who loves social interactions but also needs plenty of alone time to recharge. I also love meaningful connections and deep conversations. I loathe shallow, small talk. That factors into why I am such a transparent person. After I thought back on various situations in my life, I realized that my introverted personality was there all along, but I was too consumed with everything else to see it. Once I was able to recognize my social introversion for what it was, I was able to embrace it.

The benefit of getting to know yourself more intimately is that you are able to apply who you are and how you are to situations around you. There are specific people and certain opportunities waiting for you to be uniquely you.

Now, you answer: What have I discovered about myself that may come as a surprise to some (including myself)?

Key 3.2 What areas of my personality would I change, if I could?

Do not get this question twisted and begin to beat down the wonderful person you are. Evaluating areas that you would change about yourself should be reflective and inspiring. We all have areas that we can improve in and recognizing and being honest about them are the first steps to making any meaningful changes. Some things are hard-wired in us, but if it is an area that we would like to see growth, development or change, we can make adjustments to compensate for some of those personality traits.

An area of my personality that I have to continually work diligently at is my ability to efficiently manage my time. I used to be the person who lacked the sense of appropriating the correct length of time for an activity. Research actually shows that people underestimate the appropriate length of time a task will take by about forty percent. That was certainly the story of my life, and if I am not intentional about combating that, it will continue to be the narrative.

I was the kind of person who would assume there was enough time to retile the floor and shingle the roof just because I had five extra minutes before leaving the house. Okay, I am exaggerating, but my mind worked in a similar fashion. Maybe with those extra minutes, I would decide to quickly (but not so quickly) wash the dishes or wipe down the bathroom.

One of my greatest assets was also my greatest liability. I am naturally a productive person. I feel best when I am meaningfully producing something. On the contrary, when I am not actively participating in production, I feel like I am just wasting time. When I was a director in a child care facility, I was known for saying that there is *always* something that could be done. I used to remind my staff members that if the children were napping, they could clean their classrooms, prepare upcoming lesson plans, complete student evaluations or *anything*, but they should certainly be doing *something*. Because I am wired to think and act that way, I had a tendency to fill every moment possible with some sort of activity. It might sound good on paper to be productive but being over productive creates its own challenges. I fell victim to living in a constant state of rushing, which produced undue frustration and chronic lateness. I recall one employer inquiring about my lateness. At that moment, I had to face my reality as I responded to them and acknowledged to myself that I was simply mismanaging my time, attempting to complete far too many tasks prior to starting my work day.

After recognizing my problem, I began to take steps to override the negative qualities that were ingrained in me. I began to make detailed lists of tasks that needed to be completed. It was not enough to write them down but also appropriate realistic time constraints for completing them and then adding a buffer of time to take care of unforeseen contingencies. I had to deliberately schedule fewer activities than I thought I could handle in a specified time frame. It took conscious effort, and it *still* takes conscious effort. I am choosing to change a portion of my personality that I believe will be beneficial to pursuing my purpose in life.

When you look at areas of your personality that you would change, if you could, it is not to downplay all of the magnificent qualities that you exhibit. We have the ability to change most, if not all, parts of our personalities if we desire to do so. The desire to change should stem from a place of self-love and the longing to be the best version of yourself that you can be, not to become someone who you are not. While focusing on improving my time management skills, I did not abandon being a productive person. I simply accepted that regulating my strength in one area and improving a weakness in another area created the space for a better *me* in my totality. The same is true for you. God blessed you with a beautiful personality that is uniquely yours to serve his purpose for your life. You should keep and nurture this while working on correcting whatever flaws may exist in your character.

Now, you answer: What areas of my personality would I change, if I could?

Key 3.3 How can I intentionally put forth the time and effort to get to know myself?

You are an amazing person. The more you discover the many layers that you possess, the better you will be able to enjoy who you are and connect with those to whom you should be connected. Think about the last time you went on a date, not with a friend or significant other, but by yourself. Hanging out with those that you know and love or those who you would like to get to know and possibly love is great. There is definitely a time and space for that. Whether you are single or married, it is vital to continue to take yourself out (or stay in if you prefer) to spend time getting to know yourself better. As you grow and mature, your desires and perspectives change. That is one of the reasons that it should be a continual process of getting to know yourself.

When I first started to intentionally get to know myself, I took the brave step of going out to eat *by myself.* I always enjoyed going out to eat, actually I just loved eating, but I digress. I was accustomed to the company of someone else when I went out to eat. The very first time that I dined alone, it was completely unintentional, but it opened my heart to the idea of intentionally dining alone. It was an afternoon after I left a meeting. I was hungry and craving Red Lobster's Cheddar Bay Biscuits. I was apprehensive at first, but then I succumbed to my desire for warm biscuits. As I waited for my food and leisurely enjoyed the meal after it arrived, I perused some material from the meeting that I had just left. The experience was not bad at all. By the time that I left the restaurant, I felt accomplished. I felt like I could do *this.* Then I began to actually plan solo dining experiences.

One day someone shared her confusion on how people could dine alone. I began to say that if someone wanted to go out to eat but did not have a companion to join them, then they went out alone. I quickly corrected myself and stated that they could simply want to enjoy good food and their own company. I realized as I was speaking that dining alone was not a matter of loneliness but rather enjoying alone time.

Obviously, taking yourself out to eat is not the only means of getting to know yourself. Research the things that you are interested in and then, do them. See if it is something that looks good in theory but is not practically an interest of yours. There have been times when I packed up and headed out of the house with an idea for a wonderful alone session, and upon arrival, I decided that as good as it seemed, it was not ideal for me. One of the most important keys to getting to know yourself is reflective time. You could go out and participate in every activity that comes to mind, but if you do not spend time reflecting on your experiences and preferences, you will miss out on the benefit of dating yourself.

Now, you answer: How can I intentionally put forth the time and effort to get to know myself?

Key 3: Discover Purpose In Your Personality And Passion

Key 3.4 What do I find myself talking about most often?

Matthew 12:34b (ESV) says, "For out of the abundance of the heart the mouth speaks." Whatever you are passionate about will naturally flow out when you open your mouth. It can be something specific like love for art or something general like negativity. Think about the things that you are passionate about. What would others say that your passion is, based on what you say? Do they correlate?

I enjoy meaningful conversation, so while I tend to talk a lot, it typically has significance. Most of the time, my conversation will find its way back to God. He is absolutely *my everything*. I just love Him. Those are also two phrases that I am often caught repeating. At times, I get overwhelmed just thinking or talking about Him. When I engage with others, the joy of the Lord truly bursts through me.

One particular evening, I had a group of women over for a game night. Inevitably the conversation settled on talking about God, who He was to us, how He captured our hearts, His faithfulness through our lives and how He continued to work through our lives to touch others. As I spoke out of pure love and adoration for Him, another young lady marveled and mentioned that the way that I spoke about God was the way that people spoke about their significant others. When I pondered on what she said, I realized that it was the truth. It was not that I spoke of Him in a sensual way or as if He *was* my significant other. I merely spoke with passion, honor, and joy. God, my Father and Creator; Jesus Christ, my Lord and Savior; and the Holy Spirit, my Comforter, and Counselor, fill my heart, and it is evident when I speak.

It does not really matter who I am speaking with. God's love, Word and His heart flow from my lips even if I do not specifically say His name or quote scripture. The way that I speak prompts others to wonder where my hope and joy comes from. 1 Peter 3:15 reminds us, "But in your hearts revere Christ as Lord. Always be prepared to give an answer to everyone who asks you to give the reason for the hope that you have. But do this with gentleness and respect" (NIV).

I had the opportunity to inadvertently "give an answer" to a lovely psychologist that I met with a few times. I met with her for a parental pre-session. As a standard procedure, she began to inquire about my personal history. Over the course of a few weeks, we talked for hours, and I did the majority of the talking. As I shared some of my most intimate and traumatic experiences, she was blown away by my poise and the place of freedom that I spoke from. She was taken aback when she discovered that the healing that took place in my life was without psychological intervention. As I shared my history, I could not hold back sharing my present and future which is in Christ.

When the time came for her to explain how her practice routinely used meditation as the relaxation component of their therapy sessions, I explained our family's method. Joshua 1:8 instructs us, "Study this Book of Instruction continually. Meditate on it day and night so you will be sure to obey everything written in it. Only then will you prosper and succeed in all you do." She admitted that no one ever refused their meditation practices and she agreed that my faith was extremely important to me. I assured her that my identity as a Christian was not something that I merely checked off a box for—Female? Check; African American? Check; Christian? Check—rather it was the foundation of my life and everything that I did in it. She responded by acknowledging that my faith was ingrained in me. She mentioned that from the very first time we talked and every subsequent time that we talked, it just poured out of me and it was clearly working well for me. I did not lead her to Christ that day—or at least not to my knowledge. However, I shared the passion that filled my heart as I spoke.

Our passions are clearly heard by the things that dominate our conversations. They say that actions speak louder than words but do not let that deceive you into thinking that our words are irrelevant.

Now, you answer: What do I find myself talking about most often?

Key 3.5 What problems or issues deeply upset me?

We all have those things that extremely bother us that others may or may not notice or notice and do not care about. We are all unique and are not moved by the same issues. One person may have a burden for social injustice and another, homeless veterans. Almost all of us have a general sense of disdain or pity for problems that we see around us, but typically there is a problem or two that clinches us by the heart, grabs our attention and triggers our passion.

Brokenness—incomplete or being in a state of disarray; disorder—breaks my heart. No pun intended. Specifically, broken women break my heart. Having lived a life of brokenness for most of my life, it is an issue that I can identify and empathize with. I know the feeling of hopelessness and not loving or valuing myself. I know what it was like to continually allow others to take advantage of me because I was not secure with who I was. I walked the path of incompleteness, and now it deeply upsets me when I see other women in bondage.

Brokenness stems from a lack of knowledge of identity. Wrapped in brokenness are: low self-esteem, depression, complacency, strife, selfishness, promiscuity, heartache, idolatry, rage, impurity, hostility, and the list continues. When those issues are evident in a woman's life, the underlying root is brokenness. It is a result of not understanding and accepting her true identity in Christ. One of the scriptures that became my anchor was Colossians 2:9-10 which reminds us, "For in Christ lives all the fullness of God in a human body. So, you also are complete through your union with Christ, who is the head over every ruler and authority."

A prominent manifestation of my brokenness was the recurrence of unhealthy romantic relationships in my life. The cycle of entering unhealthy relationships, accepting and enduring toxicity and exiting just to enter yet another unhealthy relationship was the story of my adolescence and young adulthood. I subjected myself to such relationships because I thought that was as good as it got. It became the norm for me, and because I wanted the nominal attention, acceptance, affection and counterfeit love, I always conceded and consented to being treated in a derogatory manner. Despite the many problems that arose from toxic relationships, I clung to the small window of time when things were going well within the relationships.

I remember while in a toxic relationship, I discovered that a friend was in a similar relationship that was headed for destruction. I was not the most qualified person in their eyes to assess their relationship, and my concerns fell on deaf ears. My approach was as caring as I knew how to be at the time, but I admit that after witnessing their denial of their reality, my approach was intolerable. I began to get frustrated at their misinterpretation of my concern. What began as a conversation out of my affection for them later transform into a broken friendship.

Shortly after losing a friend I deeply cared about due to the conflict of pointing out their unhealthy relationship, I got a clearer picture of the true situation of the unhealthy relationship I was in myself. I realized, with more clarity, that I was in an undesirable situation, and this gave me the strength and boldness to reject and escape from the said relationship. It was in those moments that my desire peaked to see women not follow my path of brokenness. During that time, I still was not sure how to eradicate brokenness in my own life, so I was not fit to assist someone else. However; it was an issue that would one day resurface in my life with me on the side of victory.

A problem or issue that deeply upsets us does not always have to be something that we have personally experienced. It could be something that we watched a loved one endure or even something

Key 3: Discover Purpose In Your Personality And Passion

that God has placed a burden in our heart for. More times than not, those problems are connected to us and demand our empathy.

Now, you answer: What problems or issues deeply upset me?

Key 3.6 What would I spend the majority of my time doing, if money was not an option?

At some point or another, most of us have been asked a question similar to this. It could have been a high school essay topic, a team building activity at work or the prompting at a vision board party. The idea is that whatever we chose to do when money was not an option sheds light on our passion and true desires. One of the many barriers on the path to fulfillment is financial resource or ability. When that block is removed, the authenticity of what we really want and value are displayed.

When you look at people who have the financial means to gratify their desires, what does it tell you about them? In the close company of millionaires, I witnessed people who, instead of indulging in massive houses, luxury cars and fancy clothes, lived in moderate houses, drove basic cars and wore holey socks. Their choice of using their financial means was giving charitably, dining in nice restaurants and enjoying traveling. To those who may not have the means, the hypothetical question can reveal the passions and desires that are in the heart.

One day, a mentor asked me and several others the loaded question of what we would do if money was not an option. Each person took turns answering. When it was my turn to answer, I beamed with excitement. From my expression, it seemed I would be able to do those things just by saying them. My response years ago still rings true today. If money was not an option, I would spend the majority of my time helping people in various ways. Actually, I desire to be able to help people in *whatever* way they need help, whether spiritually, physically, emotionally, mentally or financially.

If there was a woman who needed help loving herself the way that God does, I would like to be there to edify her and build her up. If there was a woman who needed someone to accompany her to her doctor's appointment for emotional support, I would like to be the woman sitting next to her. If there was a woman who wanted to further her education or training but did not have the necessary information or access to resources, I would like to be there to point her in the correct direction. If there was a woman who needed a place to stay for some time while she got on her feet, I would like to be the one to offer a home to her. If a village in another country was in dire need of physical and spiritual help, I would like to be the one to fly across the world in a moment's notice to lend my support.

As I spoke those words, it ignited the idea that my dreams, which seemed too big in my head, were attainable with God, who owns all resources. God is the *source* of all resource. Do not think for a moment that God placed massive dreams and passions in your heart to lie dormant. Begin to think of those things that you would spend the majority of your time doing if money was not an option as realistic things that you have the capacity to do, empowered by God.

Now, you answer: What would I spend the majority of my time doing, if money was not an option?

Key 3: Discover Purpose In Your Personality And Passion

Key 3.7 What areas of helping others bring me the most joy?

No person is an island. We all need each other, which is why it is essential that we develop a lifestyle of helping one another. Philippians 2:4 tells us, "Don't look out only for your own interests, but take an interest in others, too." As we take an interest in others, it is vital that we identify how we are gifted and wired to help others. Those would be the ways that bring us the most joy while we do it. There are times when helping others brings inconvenience or discomfort, but overall, we should walk away with joy knowing that we brought love, life, and light to another person.

Two of the ways that I enjoy helping people that brings me joy are encouraging and giving to others. If I see a physical need that I can address, I am eager to give. Whether it is paying for a missionary's extended living expenses, sponsoring a child in a third world country or taking a homeless woman on a shopping spree, when God gives me the resources, I am eager to give it away to a cause that makes life better or easier for other people.

Just as the church service was wrapping up one day, a handicapped homeless woman wheeled inside. She was discouraged when I shared that service was ending in the next few minutes. She wanted to hear the Word of God. I invited her to lunch, explaining that we could pray, read the Bible and discuss the Word of God together. She accepted my invitation. In the diner, we prayed, wept, read the Bible and reveled in God's goodness. I encouraged her and spoke life into her even in her dark situation.

As we prayed and discussed the Bible openly, our waitress was not thrilled. She had a negative disposition, and our service was subpar. Despite her actions, I went out of my way to make sure that my reactions were full of kindness and love. When our bill came,

God placed it on my heart to give her a tip that exceeded our bill. She became a completely different person. She was humble and grateful. It opened a door for me to share God's love for her. She even shared with me what she needed prayer for. God received the glory for what He did through me for the waitress, but it was truly my pleasure.

After leaving the diner, I pushed the woman down the street in her wheelchair to the store. At the time, I still depended on God to meet my most basic needs each month but I was led to instruct her to pick out any and everything that she needed and I purchased it. By the time we left the store, it was evening. I spent several hours with the woman that I met earlier in the day. Before we departed, I made sure that she had another meal, some money to hold on to and a way to get back to the homeless shelter. That day was probably wonderful for her, but it was not one-sided. Encouraging and giving to her filled my heart with so much joy. I was so grateful for the opportunity to extend God's love and help to another person.

The bible says in Acts 20:35b, "It is more blessed to give than to receive." Time and time again, the reality of that verse is evident in our lives as we give of our time, talents and resource to others. Different areas of helping others touch each of us differently. Identify your special areas, and target those while being a blessing to others. Now, you answer: What areas of helping others bring me the most joy?

Key 3.8 How can I become a solution to a problem that I'm passionate about?

If you see something that is broken, ask yourself, "Can I fix it?" Even if you are not able to completely overhaul or eradicate a problem, evaluate whether or not you can make a significant improvement to it. Chances are if God has highlighted a problem in your life that you are passionate about, He has also equipped you to address it. Assess what experience, expertise and resources you are able to utilize to make a difference.

Given my passion for seeing broken women made whole, and my personal experience of transforming from a broken woman into a secure and complete woman, I am able to be a solution to a multitude of hurting, broken women. I am able to be the help that I needed. I learned from my past mistakes of trying to force my help onto someone that you could only help people who want help.

The key to my transformation from brokenness to wholeness was understanding who I was in Christ. I did not value myself because I lacked the understanding of how wonderful I was. It was not anything that I did that made me spectacular. The simple fact that God created me made me valuable and special. That was the notion that became more real to me as I spent more time studying the Bible. God's Word began to reveal my true identity.

Once I was secure and complete in my identity, I began to share the hope that I found with other women. The life-giving words that I read in the Bible began spilling from my lips, pouring water in the dry places of the lives of the women I connected with. I was intentional about consistently adding value to the women I encountered. When I observed women who were in toxic relationships, I did not harp on the relationship itself. I focused on sharing with the woman her value and significance. I understood that trying to convince someone that they needed to leave an unhealthy relationship was more difficult than constantly esteeming someone and letting them come to their own conclusions about their life.

More times than not, as people, we try to modify a person's fruit rather than tearing up the *root*. What I mean is that we attempt to fix all of the symptoms but ignore what the underlying problem is. The goal is to rip up the root because it will inevitably transform the removal and rottenness of the undesired fruit.

I had the pleasure of mentoring a beautiful young lady for a couple of years as she walked from brokenness to wholeness. For years, I esteemed and encouraged her and was a support to her when she needed a listening ear. I reminded her with each conversation of how precious she was. During that time, she was in an emotionally abusive relationship. Instead of ranting on how horrible her relationship was, I lovingly pointed out how loved and brilliant she was.

After years of cheering her on, she made the decision to walk away from her unhealthy relationship. It was not a result of pressure or influence but rather a realization of her value. It did not stop at only leaving an unhealthy relationship. She began to pursue God, her identity and purpose fervently. She began to dig up the root of brokenness, and her life reflected it. Now, she, in turn, pours comfort, validation, and encouragement into other young ladies who are experiencing brokenness.

Our unique experiences, expertise, and resources help equip us to be the solution to the problems that we have a passion for. No one else has lived your life, and no one else can offer the distinguishing assistance that you were created to give. No one else can reach the

Key 3: Discover Purpose In Your Personality And Passion

people that you can, and no one else can solve the problems that you were created to address in the way that you can.

Now, you answer: How can I become a solution to a problem that I'm passionate about?

KEY 4:

DISCOVER PURPOSE IN YOUR POTENTIAL AND PAYMENT

po•ten•tial | noun

1. latent qualities or abilities that may be developed and lead to future success or usefulness

pay•ment | noun

1. an amount paid

Key 4: Discover Purpose In Your Potential And Payment

Key 4.1 What comes naturally for me?

Think about your strengths for a second. If you are one of those people like I used to be, who would only come up with the same three strengths whenever I was probed to reflect on them, try this. Ask ten people for the top ten strengths or abilities that they see in you. The people who see you in action are key players in helping you identify some of those strengths that you may not easily notice. At times, we are too familiar with ourselves and do not even realize that what we naturally do is a desirable attribute that does not come naturally for everyone.

A prime example is my ability to organize. I initially did not realize the value of my natural strength in that area. It was just who I was. I *needed* things to be organized in order to function properly. Because I operated that way, I was often sought out for my organizational skills when advancement was not my intended goal.

Becoming a company director at the age of twenty-two was not something that I aimed for, but my natural gifts and abilities made room for me. Proverbs 18:16 says, "A gift opens the way and ushers the giver into the presence of the great" (NIV). In the majority of the companies that I worked for, my natural strengths and abilities, especially for leadership and organization, propelled me onto a speed track of advancement and promotion. My promotions for several key leadership positions initiated after mere days to weeks. At one company, I worked for just a couple of weeks before I received a phone call from the owner stating that they wanted me to replace the company's current director.

As I reflect, my natural strength for leadership was not-so-graciously pointed out as a kindergartener when I was deemed as *bossy* by some. Yet, even my kindergarten teacher made a note of how I helped other children and encouraged them to master some of the skills that I previously mastered. Coincidentally, I see those same attributes in my daughter. From preschool onward, she remained the teacher's helper or, in her mind, *the teacher*. Even when we go to the playground, she consistently gathers children together and instructs them on what to play with and how to play with it. The funny thing is that they all seem to pleasantly listen and follow her directions. In fact, it would appear that they enjoy taking orders from her.

Likewise, my knack for organization surfaced in my early years as well. I remember one of my favorite activities was sorting thousands of coins at a time. It was literally one of the highlights of my childhood. My aunt used to collect all of her change and I had the pleasure of sorting it when I went to visit. It was not the fact that I had the opportunity to be surrounded by fists full of money but rather the pure enjoyment of placing thousands of items into their proper place. In every aspect that I could organize and sort, I did. When I ate cereal, candies or anything that was color coordinated, I ate them one color at a time. Not only did that help set me up for future success in my career, business and ministry, it also set me up to demolish everyone at my sister's game night when we play the Separation Anxiety game.

Back when I was eating all of my red Fruit Loops first, I never would have imagined that those natural skills of organization would greatly benefit me in the future. We all have things that come naturally to us that we may not easily identify because to us, it is just who we are. Reach out to those who know you best to help you identify your strengths. You will most likely begin to see an overlap in the qualities that others see in you.

Now, you answer: What comes naturally for me?

Key 4.2 What motivates me?

What gets you going? What is it that causes you to forget to eat and not want to sleep? Think about the areas as well as the practices that cause you to be all that you can be. A motivator is something that provides a reason or stimulus to do something. Motivators can be intrinsic or extrinsic.

Intrinsic motivators stem from within a person. Either completing an activity is the person's reward, or a person receives personal satisfaction from completing an activity. This is often seen in teachers who make a nominal salary, working almost constant overtime for a thankless job. Their reward is not the prestige or abundant salary, but rather the joys of facilitating children to learn and flourish. Extrinsic motivators are birthed through outside sources. This is when a person completes an activity to receive a reward or avoid a punishment. This is often seen in sales jobs when sales associates fight to meet a quota to avoid negative performance evaluations or to greatly exceed those quotas to be awarded the top salesperson in their department. While both forms of motivation are necessary in various situations, as we strive to reach our fullest potential, intrinsic motivators are ideal and more effective at pushing us to achieve stuff than their extrinsic counterparts.

One of my greatest intrinsic motivators for reaching my fullest potential is other people. I do not mean that I do what I do for other people's approval or validation. Rather, when I contemplate how my obedience in exercising all of my God-given abilities impacts others, I am driven to reach my potential. The very fact that I am an author is a result of thinking about others. Initially, I found it difficult to start work on my first book, *Beauty for Ashes: The Transformation of my Life's Darkest Moments*. I had not done this before, and for some other reasons (which I will discuss in a later section), I felt stuck and did not know where to start from. However, I got propelled into action when I thought about generations of women that would benefit from my story long after I am gone. When I grasped the magnitude of publishing my book and its far-reaching effects, it was more than enough motivation to get started, and I spent hours each day writing my manuscript, completing the original draft in a total of seven days. Whenever I wanted to stop, the idea of those unreached women motivated me to continue and keep pushing toward the finish line.

When I talk about the various obstacles that God has empowered me to overcome, even the personal and sensitive ones such as my rape and addictions, I do so with the multitudes of women in mind who need hope. It would be easy to shrink back from doing what I was created and equipped to do because of the discomfort and possible embarrassment that it could bring. Knowing that other people, specifically women, are waiting for me to lead the way and be an example propels me.

It is not getting an award or public recognition that motivates me to live up to my fullest potential. It is the intrinsic rewards of knowing that I am impacting people's lives for the better that keeps me going. Think about the intrinsic motivators in your own life. What stimulates you to get it done?

Now, you answer: What motivates me?

Key 4.3 What is the biggest hindrance that can prevent me from reaching my fullest potential?

When you set out to do anything great, roadblocks and opposition are inevitable. At times, those roadblocks are self-imposed, and at other times they are caused by external factors. Either way, identifying what those roadblocks are and strategically knocking them down is the only way to reach your fullest potential.

Over the years, a commonality in my biggest hindrance at several points in my life was working at my jobs. My jobs in and of themselves were not a problem but the time and energy that I spent at them was the problem. I once heard Tony Gaskins say, "If you don't build your dream, someone will hire you to help build theirs." Over and over again that was my reality. By no means am I against ever having a job or working for others. I believe there is a time for everything and there are valuable skills that you can learn through employment. However, working for someone else when it is time to move forward with your own expedition can be detrimental.

After giving my employers the majority of my waking hours, I did not have the time, energy or frankly the desire to pursue my purpose and live up to my fullest potential. Even when God placed the idea in my heart to write a book, it took me over three years to begin, and that came as I was leaving my job. Around the same time that God instructed me to write a book to help women, He gave me the ministry of Secure and Complete—a ministry that exists to encourage, inspire, and support women in fulfilling God's purpose in their lives as they become secure with who they are, understanding that they are complete in Christ. Likewise, I did not have sufficient time to devote to that ministry while I was a working woman. Several aspects of unlocking my potential came when I walked away from working a nine-to-five. I was able to take my time and energy back and use it for what was most needful to actualize my potential.

Another area that commonly hinders people from reaching their fullest potential is fear. Fear is crippling. Like Franklin D. Roosevelt said in his inaugural speech, "...the only thing we have to fear is fear itself—nameless, unreasoning, unjustified terror which paralyzes needed efforts to convert retreat into advance..." Throughout the Bible, God instructed His prophets not to fear as He led them to act on the potential that He placed inside of them. He speaks the same words to us. The temptation to fear the unknown, to fear failure or even to fear what others might think of us is real.

As people, we like to know what is next and what all the details are before we proceed in doing something. We have an instinct that attracts us to seeking and maintaining security. We enjoy the convenience of comfort. Stepping out and reaching towards our fullest potential brings uncertainty. What if it does not work as planned? What if I start and cannot finish? What if I am rejected? The "What ifs" keep piling up and we become the master of hypothetical questions.

So, how do we combat fear? We combat fear by practically trusting in God. I intentionally said *practically* trusting in God because it is one thing to say with our lips that we trust in God but a completely different story to live like it. When God gave me the instruction to walk away from my job, when I was not financially prepared to, I had to put my trust in God. Quoting scripture was not going to pay my bills when my limited resources ran out. I showed that I trusted in the One who gave me the command to walk away and the potential to fulfill His plan for my life by being obedient. Basically, you combat fear by doing it anyway—whatever your *it* is—because you trust that the plans that God has for you are good (Jeremiah 29:11).

Key 4: Discover Purpose In Your Potential And Payment

I often say that God is not going to tell us to take a step of faith off of a cliff. If He is drawing us into the unknown, He is drawing us into our fullest potential. It will not be for our demise. He knows what is on the other side of our obedience and He knows what is inside of us. Do not allow fear or any hindrance to stand in the way of you reaching your fullest potential. Know that the roadblocks will come, but you have the ability to knock them down.

Now, you answer: What is the biggest hindrance for me reaching my fullest potential?

Key 4: Discover Purpose In Your Potential And Payment

Key 4.4 How can I utilize my natural talents, strengths, and motivators to realize the possibilities in my life?

They say if you don't use it, you lose it. With that being said, think about how you can realize your potential by actively cultivating and distributing your talents and strengths. Keep your motivators at the forefront of your mind as you seek to attain every possibility in your life. In Matthew 25, we can see a clear picture of what happens when we fail to utilize what God has given us.

> For it will be like a man going on a journey, who called his servants and entrusted to them his property. To one he gave five talents, to another two, to another one, to each according to his ability. Then he went away. He who had received the five talents went at once and traded with them, and he made five talents more. So also he who had the two talents made two talents more. But he who had received the one talent went and dug in the ground and hid his master's money. Now after a long time, the master of those servants came and settled accounts with them. And he who had received the five talents came forward, bringing five talents more, saying, 'Master, you delivered to me five talents; here, I have made five talents more.' His master said to him, 'Well done, good and faithful servant. You have been faithful over a little; I will set you over much. Enter into the joy of your master.' And he also who had the two talents came forward, saying, 'Master, you delivered to me two talents; here, I have made two talents more.' His master said to him, 'Well done, good and faithful servant. You have been faithful over a little; I will set you over much. Enter into the joy of your master.' He also who had received the one talent came forward, saying, 'Master, I knew you to be a hard man, reaping where you did not sow, and gathering where you scattered no seed, so I was afraid, and I went and hid your talent in the ground. Here, you have what is yours.' But his master

answered him, 'You wicked and slothful servant! You knew that I reap where I have not sown and gather where I scattered no seed? Then you ought to have invested my money with the bankers, and at my coming, I should have received what was my own with interest. So take the talent from him and give it to him who has the ten talents. For to everyone who has will more be given, and he will have an abundance. But from the one who has not, even what he has will be taken away' (Matthew 25:14-29 ESV).

The reality is that we are all stewards of the gifts, talents, and strengths that God has placed in us. The best way that we can utilize our talents is by submitting them to God to accomplish His purpose through our skills. The thing that comes to mind is singers who God has gifted with a natural talent to belt out musical notes, but they turn around and use it to exalt themselves. Or some people do what I used to do, save my gift of singing for myself. Our gifts are intended to be shared, not hidden, hoarded or distorted. Through prayer, we can seek how God would like us to best utilize our natural talents.

Now, you answer: How can I utilize my natural talents, strengths, and motivators to realize the possibilities in my life?

Key 4: Discover Purpose In Your Potential And Payment

Key 4.5 What specific costs of my time, energy and resources have I paid to achieve my goals and fulfill my purpose in life and how much am I willing to pay?

I was told that nothing in life is free and I believe it. Our goals are not an exception either. Attaining your goals, reaching your potential and living out your purpose in life will cost you. If you are going to win a prize (which, in this case, is achieving your goals), there's always a price to pay. If you have not paid anything for it, you probably are not reaping the full benefit of the life you can live. It is almost like those free trials of services that companies like to provide to you. You can enjoy it for a limited time with limited features, but if you pay the price, you can enjoy the unending abundance of all they have to offer. Which type of life would you like to live?

Everyone wants the benefits, but everyone does not want to pay the costs. One area of my purpose in life is tied to entrepreneurship. Oftentimes entrepreneurship is glorified. People highlight the freedom and flexibility that comes with it but neglect to expose some of the harsh realities associated with it.

While flexibility is a convenience, especially if you work from home, self-discipline is non-negotiable when other things in your home are competing for your attention. When I used to go to work, for the most part, my focus was on the tasks that I had to complete at work. It was in front of me. I did not have to walk past a sink full of dishes and convince myself that that moment was not the time to do it. Or even on a less productive note, I did not have my big comfy couch wooing me to sit down, kick my feet up and relax.

Apart from the higher levels of discipline that entrepreneurship requires and the benefit of flexibility of schedule, entrepreneurship requires flexibility of funds. Saying goodbye to a steady income is one of the major differences between employment and self-employment. It is one of the prices you pay for being able to name your own price (within your business to your consumers or clients). Also, when it comes to money, there could very well be times when your business is making money but you, as an owner, are not making money. Not every owner, especially early on, has the income to pay themselves after they reinvest money into their business. Even when they are able to do that, some factors can cause the amount that they can pay themselves to fluctuate. That was one of the challenges that I faced as an entrepreneur, adjusting to the difference and sometimes the lack of income flow. In order to walk in my purpose, I had to pay by means of income reduction and instability.

As if reducing my income was not enough, I also had to pay by investing the money that I already had into my business. If you are not willing to give your monetary resources to your vision and goals, why would anyone else? You have to literally and figuratively put your money where your mouth is.

Another area in which I made sacrifices was in my sleep. Because I am naturally a night owl and can easily get caught up in working for hours on end losing sleep does not affect me as much as it could affect others. Nonetheless, sleep is still something that I gave up in exchange for my purpose. There are nights when I did not go to sleep at night but rather, I went to sleep the next day when I should have woken up. What I mean is that there were times when instead of going to bed at night and waking up at six o'clock in the morning, I worked all night and finally went to bed—or rather took a morning nap—at seven o'clock in the morning. There were also times when I did not go to sleep at night because I was working, did not go to sleep during the next day because I was still working and then finally after being awake for more than thirty-six hours, went to sleep the following night.

Key 4: Discover Purpose In Your Potential And Payment

Living out your purpose will require your most valuable resource, your time. It will also vie for your energy and other resources. If you want to achieve your goals and fulfill your purpose in life, you will have to pay for it, one way or another—and usually in multiple ways.

Now, you answer: What specific costs of my time, energy and resources have I paid to achieve my goals and fulfill my purpose in life and how much am I willing to pay?

Key 4.6 What am I willing to sacrifice in order to achieve my goals?

Achieving your goals requires a give and take relationship. You are required to give yourself and your resources, and you are also required to let your pursuit of your goals take some things away. It is like the picture of the little girl who had a little teddy bear in her hands. She held on to it tightly with a dismayed countenance as her father requested it from her. He held out his hand to receive the little bear while concealing an even larger bear behind his back to surprise his daughter with. While the sacrifice that we make to achieve our goals will cost us, it will pale in comparison to what we have coming. Unfortunately, we cannot say with certainty how long the time between our sacrifice and achieving our goals will be. We also cannot negate that sacrifice by definition, is an act of giving up something valued for the sake of something else regarded as more important or worthy.

Immediately, when I think of sacrifice, Jesus' sacrifice comes to mind. He is God in the flesh, and He gave up His honored position in heaven to come down to earth to live among us and gave his life up for us. Philippians 2:5-11 states:

You must have the same attitude that Christ Jesus had. Though he was God, he did not think of equality with God as something to cling to. Instead, he gave up his divine privileges, he took the humble position of a slave and was born as a human being. When he appeared in human form, he humbled himself in obedience to God and died a criminal's death on a cross. Therefore, God elevated him to the place of highest honor and gave him the name above all other names, that at the name of Jesus every knee should bow, in heaven and on earth and under the earth, and every tongue declare that Jesus Christ is Lord, to the glory of God the Father. (Philippians 2:5-11)

As I moved closer to achieving my goals and living the purposeful life that I was called to, I realized that an area that I had to sacrifice in was in my relationships. I quickly understood that everyone that was with me could not continue to go with me. There were people who I was connected to that would hinder me from being where I needed to be and doing what I needed to do. There were attitudes and practices that festered in me when I was connected to certain people. In order to protect the purpose that I was pursuing, I had to give up what seemed good, *and actually was good at one point,* for what was better.

It was difficult to end those relationships especially when I thought that certain people would remain in my life forever. It is not to say that we will never form a relationship again but maybe we will not, and I am content with that. When I speak of letting go of relationships, I am not only referring to romantic relationships. Relationships can be of any type, personal or professional.

It is understood that when we sacrifice something, we are acknowledging that the thing that we give up is of value to us but the thing that we are seeking, as a result, outweighs what we give up. Hebrews 12:2b brings this to mind when it says, "Because of the joy awaiting him [Jesus], he endured the cross, disregarding its shame. Now he is seated in the place of honor beside God's throne." Just like Christ, we must look up to what lies ahead in order to lay down what tries to bring us temporary satisfaction in the present. We must be willing to sacrifice in order to achieve our goals.

Now, you answer: What am I willing to sacrifice in order to achieve my goals?

Key 4.7 What is the timeframe that I expect to see a return on my investments of time, energy and resources for my goals and my purpose in life; and how would I respond if I did not receive a return on my investments of time, energy and resources for my goals and my purpose in life?

After we pour our blood, sweat, and tears into something, we expect to reap the benefits of everything that we invested. The only thing is, although we may have a timetable in our minds or a projected return on our investment, we lack the ability to guarantee our outcomes. It is a good measure to set goals and deadlines. It is also imperative to keep in mind that some elements are beyond our control.

When I began writing my first book, *Beauty for Ashes*, I was sure that once I released it, all of the time, energy, and money that I put into it would manifest as hundreds to thousands of book sales and a surplus of speaking engagements. I just knew that after working so hard, I would have a larger platform to do what God created me to do—tell the world about Him and His goodness. My expectation was met by disappointment.

After releasing my book, it took me much longer than I envisioned to even sell my first 100 books. That was something that I was sure would happen on its release day based on the rave that it received leading up to its release. I thought that I would immediately begin traveling the world, speaking to women and sharing everything that God did in my life and what He wanted to do in theirs. A few speaking invitations and interviews emerged but it was nothing like the return that I expected.

What I had to keep in mind was that *Beauty for Ashes* was not only able to sell within the first year after I wrote it nor would I only be able to share my experiences from it immediately following its release. Rather, for years to come, even after I am no longer living, the testimony penned within Beauty for Ashes can continue to transform lives. And that was the purpose of me writing it to begin with. It was not about sales or exposure, but God transforming people's lives through my testimony.

The person who came to mind as I reflected on a delayed return on investment was Dr. Martin Luther King Jr. While Dr. King had a significant impact while he was living, consider the vastness of his impact in the years following his death. His mark on society did not die with him; it outlived him. He created a legacy that we still reap the benefits from today.

In the same way, it is vital to set realistic goals while understanding that there is a possibility that you might not see the full effect of your obedience to walk in your purpose. And that is okay. Our hopes should be that we are a part of something that is bigger than ourselves. We should desire for our children and their children and all of society to receive the return on our investments as we strive towards our goals and purpose in life.

Now, you answer: What is the timeframe that I expect to see a return on my investments of time, energy and resources for my goals and my purpose in life and how would I respond if I did not receive a return on my investments of time, energy and resources for my goals and my purpose in life?

KEY 5:

PURSUE YOUR PURPOSE

pur•sue | verb

1. seek to attain or accomplish (a goal), especially over a long period

pur•pose | noun

1. the reason for which something is created or exists

Key 5.1 Reflect

Reflection is key to growth. Reflection allows you to analyze and assess the overall picture as well as the details of a situation. It allows your mind to wander and your emotions to become free. Reflection works both your mind and heart simultaneously. You are able to ask and answer your own questions for clarity. Two of the best questions that you can ask yourself are, "Why?" and "How?"

The question "Why?" allows you to probe yourself beyond the surface to uncover the root, the motive, the reason behind things that you have done, your response to them and what its lasting effects are. The question "How?" challenges you to take that information and do something with it. It is not enough to recognize the root of a painful experience. The next step is discovering *how* you are going to apply what you learned to improve your future and make a difference.

Throughout this book, you were instructed to answer thirty-four questions about your past, pain, position, posture, personality, passion, potential and payment. Now is the time to reflect on those answers. If you skipped any questions, now is the time to go back to them. If you wrote down a brief thought, now is the time to go back and elaborate on it. Take your time with this step.

Do not be fearful in reflecting. Be open and honest with yourself. I promise that I will not call you up and make you stand before the class and read your responses. This is for your eyes only unless you are comfortable and compelled to share with someone else. The more vulnerable that you are in your reflection, the more beneficial this step will be for you. As you reflect, you may laugh, cry, and have "Ah-ha" moments. Do not hold back. What responses stuck out to you? Embrace it all as you take these steps in pursuing your purpose.

Key 5.2 List

After you have reflected on your responses, focus on your responses to the "How can I..." questions throughout each section. These are the blueprints for you to get from where you are to where you need or want to be. For each response, distinguish what your end result is. Next, work yourself backward listing every practical step that you would need to take in order to get to the end result. Your very last step will be your next step that you can realistically take today (or tomorrow if it is late at night.) The purpose in listing your steps is to define realistic bite-sized pieces that you can manage in order to move forward. At times, we see the end result as a vast accomplishment and get petrified by its sheer magnitude and the tons of effort it would require. But if we can break it down and manage many smaller parts of it, we can conquer what initially overwhelms us.

One of the reasons why it took me three years to write the first words or even the outline of *Beauty for Ashes* was that I was gravely intimidated by the idea of writing a *whole* book. Writing an essay, a speech or anything else seemed manageable, but an entire book was too great a task in my mind. When I began to break down my book into bite-sized chunks, I quickly realized that it was not only possible for me to write a book, but the process was much simpler than I ever could have imagined. Now, every time I write a book or coach others along as they write their own books, I start with the end in mind and break down, break down, break down.

The purpose of starting at the end is to see how each step relates to each other. We commonly write down a list of goals but fail to see how each step in our plan aligns with the process of getting from point A to point B. It can be more difficult to figure out what your first step should be than what your last step will be in order to seize your final outcome. Working backward systematically brings your first step right in front of you. It becomes something that you can accomplish immediately.

For example:

My goal for the next three to five years is to homeschool my children in an enjoyable and effective manner that is conducive for them to identify and realize their identity and purpose.

Working backwards from where I need to be to where I am:

1. Homeschool my children in a manner that works, specifically, for our family
2. Be flexible with our curriculum, schedules and practices
3. Connect with other homeschooling families to glean from their practices, resources and experiences
4. Join homeschooling groups and co-operations
5. Research homeschooling options, groups and resources
6. Connect with at least one family who has or is currently homeschooling
7. Call Jane Doe

As you work your way down the list, each step should be an extension of the previous step or answer the question of how you will accomplish the previous step. Once you get to your final step, it should be something that you are able to act on within the next twenty-four hours.

Key 5.3 Share

Once you have listed your goals along with bite-sized steps to achieve them, it is time to begin to share. Sharing is essential to your pursuit of purpose, but it could be detrimental if done incorrectly. Sharing brings a level of accountability and accessibility to the equation. When you share with others, you give them permission to directly or indirectly challenge you and hold you accountable for your words and actions. The key to sharing is to share the *right amount* with the *right people* at the *right time.*

If you want to remember (or be constantly reminded of) anything, tell your children—or any children for that matter. Children are good at bringing your plans back to your remembrance. Of course, I am not suggesting that you should go around telling random children of your plans but do know that once you share it with them, they will innocently check in on you. As I set goals for completing this book, both of my children continued to challenge me, especially if I was playing a game on my phone instead of writing. Hey, I am human, too! I have to admit, having them encourage me and knowing that they were watching my diligence in completing the task motivated me to stay the course.

Outside of motivation is the benefit of wisdom and the accountability factor. When you begin to share your plans with a couple of friends or mentors, you are able to glean wise counsel from those who you know and trust and those who may have walked a similar path. They are able to give you insight and point you to other resources. They also offer support and accountability. Having someone to cheer you on and encourage you, while still challenging you with love is an added bonus. When I was nearing the completion of my book, I had a friend say that she was going to call me the next day to see if I finished the book. She is known for giving me deadlines, and I greatly appreciate her support.

While there is a level of support that sharing with those who are closest to you can bring, there is another dimension that sharing with acquaintances and the public can bring. When you are well established in the foundation of what you are pursuing, I encourage you to reach out to acquaintances and the public. As I wrote this book, I announced its release prior to completing the manuscript. That gave me an added incentive to complete it on time. Share the big picture with anyone who will listen. Always use wisdom and discernment when sharing with others. You will find that those that you least expect to support you could be your biggest supporters. It may be that they are detached enough to appreciate what you are doing without the "Oh, that's just so-and-so" mentality, or maybe they truly have a desire to support your vision. When working on a new project, I reached out to people that I did not talk to in several months, years—or ever. Some people wanted to support me because in the past I helped them when I did not have to. They were grateful for my kindness and wanted to return the favor.

The important thing to note is that when you share, your goal is not to beg, plead or manipulate people into supporting you. You want to give people an opportunity to support you. The right people will rally around you but not if they do not have a clue that you are pursuing whatever your vision or goal is. Sharing also opens the door for networking and collaboration opportunities. Often, sharing what you are pursuing will open the door for much more than what you were expecting. It was through sharing that I became sought after for radio interviews, magazine publications and donations, even when I was not exactly looking out for them at the beginning.

When it comes to judging how much to share, with whom to share it and when to share, always consult God. He knows the hearts of every person. Another thing to keep in mind is that every person that God puts on your heart to seek to connect with will not necessarily be a person with whom you will connect with. It is possible that God allows you to share with particular people who will test your faith and determination in the face of criticism or lack of support. Some of my greatest waves of support were initiated by someone's lack of support. It conditioned my heart and challenged me to depend on God even more. Sharing offers you the benefit of added motivation, support, accountability, networking opportunities, resources and dependence and trust in God.

Key 5.4 Do

This step is a no-brainer. In order to pursue your purpose, you have to actually do something. You can have the greatest ideas and plans in the world, but if you do not act on them, you are simply a dreamer. Why stop at dreaming when you can be an achiever. Being an achiever is greater than achieving your goals for your own selfish ambition. Achievers pave the way for generations to come. Your legacy hinges on your obedience to do what God has placed inside of you to do.

Once you reach this step, it is all about taking those initial steps that you wrote down in the List section (Key 5.2). Whatever is at the bottom of your lists should be steps that you can take within the next twenty-four hours. Do not put it off. Do what you can do today, *today*!

"For everything there is a season, a time for every activity under heaven...A time to plant and a time to harvest...A time to tear down and a time to build up...A time to search and a time to quit searching" (Ecclesiastes 3:1-6a).

If I could continue in the same vein, I would say that there is a time to *plan* and a time to *do*. When you begin to execute your plan, be advised that opposition will come. It is not a matter of if, but rather when. I am reminded of Nehemiah's opposition when he was burdened with the desire to rebuild the walls of Jerusalem. In the fourth chapter of Nehemiah, he depicts the opposition that he faced. His enemies insulted him and his men, tried to stir up trouble against their mission and even attempted to kill them. Look at the diligence, persistence and determination they exuded. Let their example encourage you when opposition comes. Also, take note that Nehemiah could not accomplish his mission alone.

Also our enemies said, "Before they know it or see us, we will be right there among them and will kill them and put an end to the work." When our enemies heard that we were aware of their plot and that God had frustrated it, we all returned to the wall, each to our own work. From that day on, half of my men did the work, while the other half were equipped with spears, shields, bows and armor. The officers posted themselves behind all the people of Judah who were building the wall. Those who carried materials did their work with one hand and held a weapon in the other, and each of the builders wore his sword at his side as he worked. (Nehemiah 4:11b, 15b-18)

There is not much more left to be said for this stage. Either you put your plan to work or you settle for leaving this earth with pinned up potential. Your life and the lives that follow you will be fulfilled by the former rather than the latter.

Key 5.5 Check

Whether you are in school, employed or pursuing your purpose, evaluating where you are and how you are doing is essential. During this stage, you want to assess where you are in the grand scheme of your purpose. Do not only look at how many things you have checked off of your list of things to do but also your effectiveness and the outcomes of completing those tasks. Evaluate your own strengths and weaknesses throughout the process.

Checking to see how things are going is not a one-time thing. As you progress through the process of pursuing your purpose, you should periodically conduct evaluations. When I first wrote the business plan for my women's ministry, Secure and Complete, I sat on it. I was empowered and on fire to check that item off my list of things to do, but then my momentum faltered. I was not consistently making strides in the direction of my goals. Checking in allows you to assess whether or not you are consistently moving forward.

The success of continually checking items off of your list can be invigorating, but it cannot stop there. You have to go a step further and evaluate how successful the strides that you are making are to the overall purpose that you are pursuing. The last thing you want to do is to occupy your time, energy, and resources with futile tasks. Do not be a *Martha* when you can be a *Mary*.

As Jesus and the disciples continued on their way to Jerusalem, they came to a certain village where a woman named Martha welcomed him into her home. Her sister, Mary, sat at the Lord's feet, listening to what he taught. But Martha was distracted by the big dinner she was preparing. She came to Jesus and said, "Lord, doesn't it seem unfair to you that my sister just sits here while I do all the work? Tell her to come and help me." But the Lord said to her, "My

dear Martha, you are worried and upset over all these details! There is only one thing worth being concerned about. Mary has discovered it, and it will not be taken away from her" (Luke 10:38-42).

All of your efforts should be purposeful and contribute to your end goal. At times, the contribution that a particular task will make is simply showing you what not to do. When you have those moments, treasure them because they may, in fact, be more valuable than the things that you do correctly. When I used a publisher for my first book, I ran into some challenges. Instead of pouting about it when things did not pan out the way that I expected, I captured those instances as learning opportunities. Those very challenges became prominent points in my mind as I began to build my own publishing company.

Lastly, remember to check yourself. Assess the areas that you are excelling in and the areas that you could use more work in. Sometimes it may not be an intellectual deficiency. It could be a mental or behavioral adjustment that you need to make. You could notice that if you do not set a strict schedule that you do not accomplish your goals. It could be vice versa, where you notice that strict schedules detract from your overall productivity. As you evaluate yourself, remember that you are human, so be kind to yourself.

You would not find it acceptable for your employer to fail to evaluate your performance, so do not accept it from yourself. The benefit of checking in on your progress is valuable and should be taken advantage of consistently. It helps you to gauge where you are going by assessing where you are.

Key 5.6 Repeat

You did it! You accomplished that goal; you changed your career; you started your business; you wrote your book; you started your family; you led that ministry; you moved to that country; you received that degree. Now what? As you know, life goes on after you attain a goal or milestone. The beauty is that we were not created for a singular purpose, which once we discover and fulfill, that is it, we can now put our feet up and just glide aimlessly through the rest of our life. Wrong! That is not our original design.

Often when we hear people talk about discovering purpose or pursuing purpose, they say it as if it is only one thing. The truth is that we were created with purposes and our purposes are multifaceted. I believe there is an overarching purpose that we are all called to, which is to glorify God and to make disciples of Jesus Christ, but the way in which we carry out those purposes are unique to us. In every season and every situation, God has a purpose for us. When your car breaks down purely so that you can have a life-changing conversation with the mechanic, that is purpose being fulfilled. The key is to be able to recognize that purpose in every area of your life and maximize your opportunities to actively pursue it.

Throughout this book, you were able to discover purpose in your past, pain, position, posture, personality, passion, potential and payment. Each of those areas is essential. God can and wants to use every part of you—the good, the bad, the ugly and indifferent. As you continue to live out your purpose in life periodically repeat these steps. Life's experiences and incremental knowledge have a way of changing our perspectives. What may have applied to you at one particular point in your life could drastically change at another point. As long as you are living, continue pursuing purpose.

ABOUT THE AUTHOR

The question of *why* Kyra Lanae does what she does is more important than the question of *who* she is. Kyra Lanae's relationship with Jesus Christ and desire to please her Father, God, is the driving force behind everything she does. Whether writing books, speaking publicly, mentoring or encouraging others in her daily life, her heart's desire is to help people. As for *who* she is, Kyra Lanae is a Christ-follower and mother native to Philadelphia, Pennsylvania. Kyra Lanae currently resides in the Philadelphia Suburbs with her two wonderful children, Cameron Nasir and Sabrina Marie.

Kyra Lanae is an internationally known author, publisher, and dynamic, inspirational, and authentic speaker who empowers women worldwide in the areas of identity, purpose, relationships, parenting, ministry and writing. Kyra is the author of *Beauty for Ashes: The Transformation of my Life's Darkest Moments* and *Pursuing Purpose: 5 Keys to Fulfilling Your God-Given Purpose.* Kyra is also the founder and president of Glorious Works Publishing.

Kyra delivers wisdom and practical application as she shares her successes and failures transparently. Kyra is wise beyond her years which enables her to relate to women of all ages, from Millennials to Baby Boomers. When she writes or speaks, you are sure to walk away with a new perspective, unearthed courage or reasonable next steps. She is like a gold miner of the heart, digging up precious treasures in the women whom she addresses. As women's identities, mindsets, and lives are transformed, so are their families, ministries, careers, businesses and communities. As Kyra pours strength into women, she motivates them to continue the cycle of strengthening other women. Women glean from the faith, hope and love that Kyra exudes as she walks women through her journey of overcoming rape, divorce, addictions and suicidal thoughts, just to name a few and pursuing her God-given purpose in life.

Kyra Lanae has had the honor of being featured in *31 Wife in Training*, an international Christian Women's magazine based out of Cape Town, South Africa. Kyra has also been a special guest and speaker for ministries and organizations including Gathering Connection Fellowship and Simplicity HealthStyle. Kyra's refreshing spirit, wisdom, influence and contribution has opened the door for recurring invitations from every organization with whom she has partnered.

Kyra Lanae can be reached via email at admin@kyralanae.com or directly through her website, kyralanae.com. For booking, please visit kyralanae.com/booking. For publishing, please visit gloriousworkspublishing.com.

More Titles by Kyra Lanae

- Beauty for Ashes: The Transformation of my Life's Darkest Moments
- Pursuing Purpose Workbook: 5 Keys to Fulfilling Your God-Given Purpose

Coming Soon by Kyra Lanae

- Oh, the Things That They Say: Life Lessons to Learn From the Silly Things That Kids Say
- Moment by Moment Journal: Living Life After Losing a Loved One
- Life Lessons for Kids Series: Will You Play With Me?
- Purely Single: How to Successfully and Enjoyably Experience Purity and Singleness